Outsourcing the American Dream

Outsourcing the American Dream

Pain and Pleasure in the Era of Downsizing

Christopher M. England

Writers Club Press
San Jose New York Lincoln Shanghai

Outsourcing the American Dream
Pain and Pleasure in the Era of Downsizing

Writers Club Press
an imprint of iUniverse.com, Inc.

For information address:
iUniverse.com, Inc.
5220 S 16th, Ste. 200
Lincoln, NE 68512
www.iuniverse.com

ISBN: 0-595-20148-2

Illustrations by Dennis England

Printed in the United States of America

Dedication

Dedicated to those Americans who see each day as a clean slate, a fresh chance to write a new script and seize new opportunities to overcome the obstacles to the American Dream.

Most of all, to my father, David, and my sister-in-law, Kim Ellen, both victims of corporate mismanagement and downsizing in the 1990s.

Contents

Acknowledgements

Even though I take full responsibility for the rather unconventional thoughts and ideas expressed in this book, I must express my deepest admiration and gratitude to the following:

To my family members and closest friends who gave me support and encouragement, believing what I was doing would make a positive, long-lasting impact on our society. Thanks for putting up with my long hours of research and preparation.

To the MBA faculty of Franklin University in Columbus, Ohio who gave me as much opportunity to shape the MBA Program with my thoughts and ideas as I gave them to shape my life with theirs. The self-assessment instruments used in the program, particularly the Herrmann Brain Dominance Instrument and the Myers-Briggs Type Indicator, were invaluable self-discovery tools. Is it any wonder the Franklin University MBA Program, featuring an artist-in-residence, is cited as a dramatic development in creative problem solving by Ned Herrmann in his book *The Whole Brain Business Book?*

To John Clemens and Douglas Mayer, authors of *The Classic Touch,* who inspired me to free myself of modern-day mindsets to see the world of business in unconventional ways. Additionally, I owe a great deal of gratitude to the numerous avant-garde artists and musicians that help me daily to think outside the box and to think creatively. The acclaimed Swiss surrealist artist, Paul Klee, stated it best:

"Art does not reproduce what we see. It makes us see."

To my former managers—some good and some bad—who taught me how to succeed in the world of business. From the good managers, I learned how to do the right things right simply because I did what they did. From the bad managers, I learned how to do the right things right simply because I did the opposite of what they did. Thanks for giving me the opportunity to learn not only from my own successes and failures, but from yours as well.

To the many Americans accepting challenges and taking initiatives to overcome the obstacles to the American Dream. Thank you in advance for joining the crusade and spreading your wings. This book is written for those who have yet to fulfill their dreams, but, nevertheless, feel they have at their disposal an abundance of resources with which to fulfill their dreams.

Introduction

"The only limits are, as always, those of vision."
—*James Broughton, poet and avant-garde filmmaker*

Shattered Dreams

There is nothing more difficult to take in hand, more perilous to conduct, or more uncertain in its success, than to take the lead in the introduction of a new order of things.

This passage written by Niccolo Machiavelli in his sixteenth-century masterpiece, *The Prince*, brings an interesting perspective to a modern-day paradox: in a time of unprecedented prosperity, why have millions of Americans lost faith in their ability to prosper? Why do millions of Americans fail to achieve financial abundance in a nation where unlimited economic opportunity abounds?

Yes, Machiavelli's words are timeless words for rapidly changing times. Today's business environment is chaotic, to say the least—continually shifting political and social conditions, market dislocations, rapid technological obsolescence, and turbulent international competition. The most common response to such fragmentary business patterns has been corporate downsizing. Middle America is under siege…

According to data available from the United States Bureau of Labor Statistics, roughly 2 million jobs were eliminated annually between 1979 and 1999 as a result of corporate downsizing, or approximately 40 million jobs in total. While it's true the economy created more jobs than were eliminated during this period, United States Department of Labor figures indicate that only thirty-five percent of laid-off full-time workers wound up in equal or better paying jobs. Millions more are trapped in un-satisfying careers, unable to advance within their companies or move to another. Moreover, with the evolution of high-tech materials and production technologies, unskilled and semi-skilled manufacturing jobs have all but disappeared. Additionally, many of the new service jobs that have replaced the well-paying manufacturing jobs are low-paying or part-time. What is more unsettling, the odds of losing **your** job are one in ten! YOU ARE NOT IMMUNE. Is it any wonder job security and career satisfaction rank number one and two, respectively, on the list of concerns of middle-income Americans?

The impact of downsizing on the individual can be devastating: intense anxiety and depression and a reduction in self-worth and competence. For many Americans, the very word can sound like a death sentence. I should know. In 1995, my father, David, and my sister-in-law, Kim Ellen, with nearly fifty years' combined insurance industry experience, were stripped of their livelihoods. While the family was beginning to cope with the situation, we combed stores for books to help us adjust to our new life. Most books on the market suggested following a model originated by Dr. Elisabeth Kübler-Ross in her 1969 book, *On Death and Dying*. According to her model, people evolve through a series of stages—denial, anger, bargaining, depression, and final acceptance—as they confront their own mortality or that of a loved one. Such books claim that her model is just as applicable to the corporate world as it was to a clinical environment. Many were useful—they helped explain what had happened to us. Unfortunately, none explained *why* it had happened to us and what specifically we could do to recover, and, more importantly, what our nation as a whole could do to recover. I wanted to write the book my family desperately needed to read. *Outsourcing the American Dream* is that book.

There are two types of individuals in every situation—*Problem Perceivers* and *Opportunity Perceivers*:

- Problem Perceivers perceive change as a problem. Although they may have realistic fears about the future, these individuals fail to take full responsibility for their situation and fail to actively contribute to their own recovery. They often allow others to control their destinies.

- Opportunity Perceivers perceive change as an opportunity. Although they may have realistic fears about the future, these individuals take full responsibility for their situation and actively contribute to their own recovery. They rarely allow others to control their destinies.

While seemingly revolutionary, my message is simple: if you perceive change as a problem, solve it; if you perceive change as an opportunity, take advantage of it. The fact is, we must take control of our lives and live our dreams. If we do not, someone else will.

Clouded Visions

Many managers have clung to old ways of thinking, old formulas, and old ideologies, which no longer seem to fit with the emerging values, technologies, and geo-economic relationships of today's business environment. What's worse, too many managers have jumped on the re-engineering bandwagon, blindly applying new organizational "paradigms" with names like business process improvement, concurrent engineering, self-directed work teams, strategic networks, and total quality management. The terms may vary, but the objective is the same: to produce improved financial performance, greater customer satisfaction, or enhanced organizational effectiveness. These results only can be achieved with continuous, fundamental changes in leadership. Steven Wynn, Chief Executive Officer of Mirage Resorts, stated it best:

> "You can't make money cutting costs, only by increasing revenue…sometimes good leadership requires putting the short-term concerns aside for the long-term good."

Unfortunately, many organizations have downsized without much thought as to the long-term strategic importance of leadership. In search of a quick fix to the financial performance problem, these organizations have indiscriminately cut layers of management and technical expertise to reduce labor costs. There are numerous examples of this short-term, near-sighted corporate behavior. Siemens unwisely spun off its core microchip manufacturing processes and technical expertise to savvy global competitors. Strategic alliances between American and foreign manufacturers often wound up (and still wind up) with the American manufacturers *giving* their technology away. While these companies have gained in the short term, they've lost over the long haul.

America still leads the world in science and technology invention. Unfortunately, America lags in innovation—getting our inventions to market. So who's making the profits from *our* inventions? *The Japanese, of course.* While we've been trying to win with headline-grabbing homeruns (breakthroughs), the Japanese have been beating us with singles (incremental improvements). To survive and prosper in today's global economy, American corporations must learn to develop a balance between invention and innovation, between breakthroughs and incremental improvements.

The Timeless Language Of Leadership

To lead, or not to lead:
that is the question....

Kings, prophets, and warriors served as symbols of leadership in the Greek and Roman classics. Greek concepts of leadership, both good and bad, were exemplified by Achilles and Agamemnon in Homer's *Iliad*. Plutarch compared the traits and behaviors of actual Greek and Roman leaders in *Lives of the Noble Grecians and Romans*. For early American essayists, "the industrial man" symbolized leadership. The subject of leadership is not limited to the classics of Western literature. It was as much interest to Confucius and Sun Tzu as to Homer and Plutarch. Sun Tzu, in *The Art of War*, argued for purposeful, information-centered, and flexible leadership. In their book, *The Classic Touch: Lessons in Leadership from Homer to Hemingway*, John Clemens and Douglas Mayer illustrate the key business-related points of many of these works. While I do not agree completely with Clemens and Mayer's interpretations and conclusions, *The Classic Touch*, nonetheless, offers critical leadership insights.

Today's leaders need to look back to see old patterns—the enduring principles of the human condition, the experience of others, and the lessons of history. There are patterns of success and there are patterns of failure. It's wise to heed the insights of the classics because others have struggled with the same leadership problems we face today. Others have worried about what now worries us. Others have contemplated the thoughts, both positive and negative, that occur to those who look ahead to seize new potentials. Whether they're building teams, designing organizations, planning competitive actions and strategies, or using power and influence, today's leaders need to learn the timeless language of leadership and need to develop unconventional frameworks for making reasoned leadership decisions. It's time for America to unlock its full potential by rethinking the way it thinks…or the American Dream will be lost forever…

Where there is no vision, the people perish.
—Proverbs 29:18

Chapter 1

Breaking The Ties That Bind: The Psychological Effects Of Downsizing On The Individual

"What a man can be, he must be. This need we call self-actualization."

—Abraham Maslow, American psychologist

Downsizing Is A Disease: Anorexia And Bulimia

Downsizing may reduce corporate costs and take advantage of technological advances, but it has its dangers. Many organizations, in their efforts to cut out the fat, often cut out the muscle as well. What's worse, many organizations engage in a "binge and purge" process, swallowing up competitors to increase market share, only to turn around and force themselves to "throw up" thousands of workers. Both anorexia and bulimia can devastate employee morale and hamper the organization's ability to grow. Large corporations that lay off managers and professionals to slash costs, *especially in the face of rising profits and executive salaries,* risk losing the loyalty of the employees that remain. The phrase "our employees are our most valuable asset" has become "our employees are our most disposable asset." Downsizing may cut costs in the short term, but at the expense of the people who have the potential to create value for the organization in the long term. Moreover, the very people who are destroying the long-term competitiveness of our companies are rewarded because they produce results in the short term.

Plutarch's *Life of Alexander the Great* and Maslow's Hierarchy of Needs Theory

Key learning from *Life of Alexander The Great:* *Like Machiavelli's* The Prince, *Plutarch's* Life of Alexander the Great *deals extensively with the subject of conquering and absorbing rival kingdoms (mergers and acquisitions). According to John Clemens and Douglas Mayer in their book,* The Classic Touch: Lessons in Leadership from Homer to Hemingway:

> *The crucial point is to recognize that the first effect of a merger is profound people trauma, and that the wounds can be slow to heal. Employees are traumatized because their psychological contract has been broken…This defensive behavior must be neutralized by an explicit strategy that ensures continuity, demonstrates respect for the values and mores of the acquired organization, and crisply identifies the new organization's goals. Only then can all employees understand exactly where they fit in under the "new arrangement."* (Clemens, John K., and Douglas F. Mayer. **The Classic Touch: Lessons in Leadership from Homer to Hemingway.** 2nd ed. Lincolnwood, IL: NTC/Contemporary Books,1999. Used with permission of The McGraw-Hill Companies.)

Maslow's Hierarchy of Needs

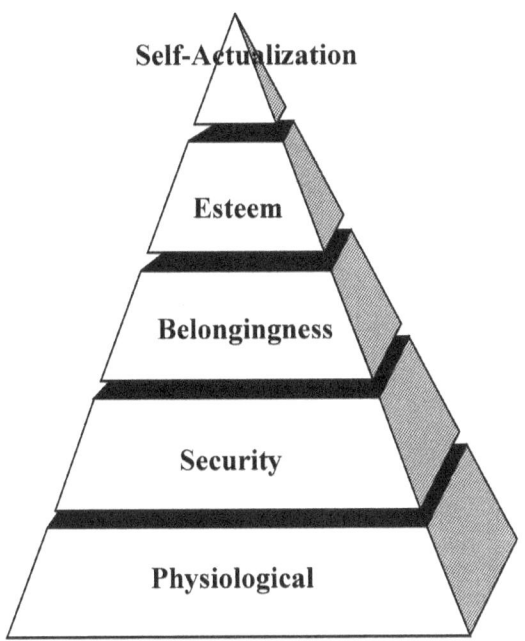

Abraham Maslow's Hierarchy Of Needs

Need theories suggest that individuals are motivated to satisfy certain physical and psychological needs. Abraham Maslow's Hierarchy of Needs is one such theory. According to Maslow, human beings have a variety of needs, some more fundamental or basic than others. Maslow grouped these needs into five categories, arranged in a hierarchy from lower *deficiency* needs (physiological, security, belongingness) to higher *growth* needs (esteem, self-actualization). Deficiency needs dominate behavior until they are satisfied. Once deficiency needs are satisfied, an individual begins the move up the hierarchy to focus on growth needs.

Downsizing Affects Movement Up The Hierarchy

If an employee has food, clothing, shelter, security, companionship, and self-esteem, only then will he or she be motivated by self-improvement. If, on the other hand, employees are concerned about job security, they're not going to be concentrating on improving financial performance, customer satisfaction, or organizational effectiveness. They'll be worrying about themselves—their own fear, frustration, and stress. Employees do not inherently put the company first. Thus, an employee will not be motivated to self-actualization if the preceding four levels of needs are not satisfied. *All motivation comes from within the employee.*

The perceived deprivation of job security has behavioral consequences. Think of an employee who has been in the same job with the same company for years. Both the job and the company provide a source of identity. Downsizing gnaws away at the various organizational subcultures and the relationships among them, destroying an employee's source of identity. A "self-actualized" or growing employee may regress to lower level needs, since a previously satisfied lower-level set of needs has become deficient again. Not feeling secure, the employee starts to think about the income she may lose and to worry about her mortgage and her ability to provide for her family. The employee asks herself daily *will I be next?* The impact on the employee can be devastating: intense anxiety and depression and a reduction in self-worth and competence. This, in turn, may lead to reduced productivity and increased absenteeism and turnover. It does not have to end this way.

Using The Hierarchy To Secure Commitment And Involvement

Both lower deficiency needs and higher growth needs can be satisfied in an organizational setting. First, physiological needs can be satisfied by providing adequate ventilation and comfortable temperatures as well as an adequate base salary to provide food, water, and shelter. Second, security needs can be satisfied by providing adequate fringe benefits, job security, and a safe work environment. Third, belongingness needs can be satisfied by providing an atmosphere for positive relationships with coworkers, work groups, management, and the corporation itself. Fourth, esteem needs can be satisfied by providing recognition, increases in responsibility and status, and credit for valuable contributions to the organization. Fifth, self-actualization needs can be satisfied by providing opportunities to grow, to be creative, and to acquire training for challenging assignments and advancement. If the company satisfies an employee's basic needs for the right working environment, the right tools, and the right leadership, the employee will provide the commitment and the involvement.

Specifically, organizations considering a reduction in staff must

- Acquire, motivate, develop, and retain those who can *lead* people and *manage* assets and resources. People like to be lead, not managed. Provide your employees with direction, informational support, and training.
- Develop new rewards to replace job security. One way to encourage growth and development is to make existing jobs more challenging. Another way is to encourage lateral transfers to other jobs or departments to promote the development of new skills. Emphasize learning, while keeping in mind that failure is part of the learning process. Organizations can earn employee loyalty by

increasing employees' skills through education and training and keeping them informed of developmental opportunities throughout the organization.

- Develop uniform policies and implement them uniformly throughout the organization. If you make staff reductions on the basis of performance in one area of the organization, it is not wise to use years of service as the criterion in another area of the organization. (Unless, of course, you enjoy wasting corporate assets defending your actions in court.)

- Improve communication. Prepare all members of the organization in advance with informative departmental briefings, memos, newsletters, and videos. Focus on the competitive forces driving the need for organizational change and provide a strategic plan for regenerating an environment of high-energy and excitement. Do not allow the grapevine to control your efforts.

- Redesign performance management and reward systems to eliminate "turf wars" between organizational departments competing for limited resources. Each department must have a clear understanding of what the organization is trying to achieve. Remember, those who stand to lose power and position may stand in the way of success.

- Put the word "fun" back into the work environment and back into everyone's vocabulary.

Dealing effectively with the problem of downsizing can enhance productivity and the retention of valued employees.

Chapter Theme Song: "*Walk On*," Boston

Chapter 2

Enough Already!

"If you do what you've always done, you'll get what you've always gotten."

—Anonymous

The most common response to declining financial performance has been downsizing and the trend is gaining steady momentum as our economy continues the shift from an industrial/manufacturing base toward a service/trade base. More than 40 million jobs were eliminated between 1979 and 1999 as a result of corporate downsizing.

Cutting People Alone Is Inadequate

Cutting people does not, in itself, produce improved financial performance, greater customer satisfaction, or enhanced organizational effectiveness. These results only can be achieved with continuous, fundamental changes in core business processes. Unfortunately, many organizations have downsized without much thought as to the long-term strategic importance of core business processes. In search of a quick fix to the financial performance problem, these organizations have indiscriminately cut layers of management and technical expertise to reduce labor costs.

High-performing organizations, on the other hand, have made reductions in staff only after careful consideration of the long-term impact of the change on financial performance, customer satisfaction, and organizational effectiveness. What is more important, high-performing organizations do not focus on returns to the company without considering returns to the customer. In addition, high-performing organization's do not focus on returns to the customer without considering returns to the employee. Yes, it's true the customer is the reason for a company's existence; however, it is the employee who *provides* service to the customer. If the company does not satisfy an employee's basic needs for the right working environment, the right tools, or the right leadership, the customer never will be first in their minds. When they ought to be thinking about the customer, they'll be thinking about their own fear, frustration, and stress.

Right Working Environment, Right Tools, Right Leadership

The old social contract of corporate loyalty and lifelong job security is dead. The expiration of this contract has resulted in a lack of motivation in the workplace, absenteeism, and turnover (as well as fear, frustration, and stress). High-performing organizations have attempted to regenerate an environment of high-energy and excitement with a new social contract: "We will not provide lifelong job security; however, we will provide the right working environment, the right tools, and the right leadership. You will provide the commitment and involvement." It appears to be working.

Self-directed work teams are becoming the basic building block of the high-performing organization. These corporations are organizing around teams to encourage the development of the skills and abilities necessary to respond to changing customer needs and to be the first to innovate (introduce a new product or invention to the market). These organizations realize the company who successfully innovates first will earn 70% of the revenues over the life cycle of the invention or product. These organizations also are aware that countless invention or product imitators will enter the market by copying or improving the invention or product, and launching it. Thus, these organizations constantly search for better ways to serve the market's needs. Research and development, manufacturing, and marketing are united as a series of inter-related processes under the same product or service umbrella, rather than as distinct functional departments. A spirit of continuous improvement permeates the entire organization. These organizations encourage every employee to learn new skills, try new approaches, or think or act in a different way. Each employee is viewed as a source of fresh ideas, new perspectives, and original applications.

It's Not Good Enough To Do What You've Always Done Anymore

Unfortunately, many organization's structures and systems suppress, rather than nourish, continuous improvement. The restrictive structures and systems result in repetitive, routine, boring jobs that undercut employee satisfaction, involvement, and commitment. Thus, the structures and systems of many organizations must be re-designed to provide the flexibility and freedom to continuously improve financial performance, customer satisfaction, and organizational effectiveness. Specifically, you must

- Begin by hiring the right people. Individuals should be selected for what they bring to the team. Make sure there is a match between the employee and the organization and the employee and the job. Let each employee make a well-informed decision about whether the organization (and the job) is right for them. (You also must begin by firing the wrong ones. Keeping non-productive or under-performing employees drains the company of value.)

- Perform the core business processes in house and outsource the ancillary tasks. Never outsource the core business processes. (Unless, of course, you want to train your competition.) Many American manufacturers have done just this by subcontracting or outsourcing entire subassemblies, and the necessary technology, to third party or foreign manufacturers. Additionally, identify processes you can grow into consulting services and profit centers, allowing such processes to provide added revenue to the company.

- Analyze the skill mix of your labor force to ensure your human assets are matched with the demands of the task. Employees with limited skills have limited opportunities to expand your business and serve your customers.

- Redesign performance management and reward systems to ensure workers are compensated in the most appropriate ways.

- Involve everyone—including your contingent labor force—by giving them the information they need to understand their part in the larger task. All employees require a clear understanding about what the organization is trying to achieve. Each employee must be prepared for the organization's anticipated future.

- Get out of the corner office and meet your customers, employees, and suppliers often. Explain the roles of employees and suppliers, the direction of the company, and the importance of customers.

- Know at all times where you are going, but force your competitors to guess where you are going, with a heavy penalty for guessing wrong. A moving target is more difficult to hit.

- Do unto your employees as you would have them do unto your customers. Afterall, your employees will treat your customers exactly as you treat them. You cannot treat your employees poorly and expect them to treat your customers well.

- In short, provide the freedom and flexibility to make decisions relevant to job activities, encourage and welcome new ideas on how to improve the company, and provide the necessary resources to get the job done. It's not good enough just to "right-size" anymore.

"If there is something that you can do, even dream that you can—begin it! Boldness has mystery and power and magic in it."
—Johann Wolfgang Von Goethe, German novelist and philosopher

Sophocles' *Antigone* and The Ohio State Leadership Studies

Key learning from *Antigone:* *Similar to Homer's* Iliad *in plot, Sophocles'* Antigone *is dominated by a conflict between the drama's heroine, Antigone (which literally means "born to oppose"), and Creon, regent of Thebes. The confrontation between Antigone and Creon over the burial of Antigone's brother, Polynices, and the tragic consequences of that confrontation, forms much of the drama's plot. When Antigone publicly defies Creon's orders ("challenges the system") and buries her brother, Creon fails to achieve a balance between Antigone's individual needs for closure and lamentation, and the needs of the city (organization) for strong leadership and stability. Creon's inflexibility ultimately results in the suicides of the imprisoned Antigone, and his betrothed son, Haemon, who killed himself upon her death.*

Researchers at The Ohio State University surveyed industrial and military leaders to study hundreds of dimensions of leader behavior. They identified two major behaviors, called *consideration* and *initiating structure.* Consideration is a type of leader behavior that describes the extent to which a leader is sensitive to subordinates, respects their feelings and ideas, and establishes mutual trust. Initiating structure is a type of leader behavior that describes the extent to which a leader is task oriented and directs subordinates' work activities toward goal achievement.

Consideration and initiating structure are independent of each other; a leader may have any of four styles reflecting the four combinations of consideration and initiating structure. The Ohio State research found that the high consideration/high initiating structure leader style achieved better performance and greater satisfaction than the other leader styles. These leaders balanced individual (consideration) with organizational (initiating structure) needs.

Robert Blake and Jane Mouton's Managerial Grid is similar to the Ohio State Studies except that consideration behavior is called "concern for people" and initiating structure behavior is called "concern for production." Blake and Mouton, both industrial and organizational psychologists, found that the high concern for people/high concern for production leader style achieved better performance and greater satisfaction than the other leader styles.

Chapter 3

Certainty And Control: The Psychological Forces Behind Downsizing

"The only certainty is that nothing is certain."

—*Pliny the Elder, Roman naturalist*

Why Are America's Largest Corporations Downsizing?

In the first chapter, I introduced Abraham Maslow's Hierarchy of Needs Theory to describe the psychological effects of downsizing on the individual. Although Maslow's theory provides a sound explanation for the effects of downsizing on the individual, it does not provide a sound explanation for the psychological forces fueling the corporate movement toward downsizing. For this, we need to turn to Henry Alexander Murray's Manifest Needs Framework.

Niccolo Machiavelli's *The* Prince and Murray's Manifest Needs Framework

Key learning from *The Prince: Like Plutarch's* Life of Alexander the Great, *Machiavelli's* The Prince *deals extensively with the subject of conquering and absorbing rival kingdoms (mergers and acquisitions). Dominated by Machiavelli's obsession with the uses and abuses of power,* The Prince *serves as an instruction manual for acquiring and maintaining the political power necessary to run kingdoms (organizations). Machiavelli acknowledges that people have a basic need or desire to acquire and maintain power, and upholds the legitimate role power plays in determining the success or failure of a leader.*

Like Maslow's needs hierarchy, the manifest needs framework assumes people have a set of needs that motivates behavior; however, the mechanisms by which needs operate are somewhat more complex in this view. American psychologist Henry Alexander Murray suggests that several categories of needs—achievement, affiliation, and power, for example—are important to most people and that any number of needs may be operating in varying degrees at the same time. That is, multiple needs motivate behavior simultaneously rather than in some preset order, or hierarchy.

Leadership is the ability to influence other people toward the attainment of organizational goals. Thus, leadership involves the use of power. *Power,* according to Murray, *is defined as any attempt to control one's environment and to influence or direct other people.* Murray's definition of power implies that people have a basic need or desire to be in control of their environments. Appropriate environmental conditions are necessary for such a need to manifest itself in behavior. The need for power manifests itself whenever any, or all, of the following conditions are present: ambiguous decisions or goals; rapid environmental, organizational, personal, or technological change; and scarce resources. People use power and other resources when these conditions are present to maintain control, to obtain a preferred outcome, and to reduce uncertainty.

Murray also was one of the first to recognize resistance as a form of power. People typically resist a change they believe will take away something of value. A proposed change in job design, structure, or technology may lead to a perceived loss of control. This perceived loss of control is perhaps the biggest obstacle to organizational change.

The rapid environmental, political, and technological changes of the past decade have taken away two things of value—certainty and control. Many corporate leaders long for a return to more stable economic times, when American corporations dominated the marketplace. In the three decades following World War II, American corporations were the only players in town; they could sell anything they could produce, even if the product or service offering was second rate. There wasn't any need to change the proven business practices of the post-war economy. American corporations *controlled* the marketplace and were *certain* of their continued future success. They adopted aggressive merger and acquisition strategies to fuel growth and to expand market share in "mature" industries.

By the 1980's, new international players employing avant-garde business practices had joined the economic game. Decades of certainty and control disappeared in the blink of an eye. The new players maintained leaner and more adaptable organizational structures than their American rivals. American corporations were saddled with the multi-layered, bureaucratic organizational structures, which had served them so well in stable economic times. Such Byzantine bureaucracies quickly became too complex and too cumbersome to manage in rapidly-changing economic times. American corporations had to develop new strategies in order to remain competitive and to cut costs. Cost-cutting efforts led to recommendations for eliminating layers of management, centralizing some duplicated functions, and increasing automation. In effect, American corporations turned to the power of downsizing to maintain control over their environments and to reduce uncertainty.

"The certainties of one age are the problems of the next."
—Richard Henry Tawney, English economic historian

Chapter 4

Downsizing's Upside:
The Creation Of New Industries

"In the middle of every difficulty lies opportunity."
—Albert Einstein, German-born American mathematical
physicist and Nobel Prize winner (1921)

Human Resources Consulting And Benefits Outsourcing

Outsourcing of benefits administration operations in many organizations has transformed the human resources function. Such outsourcing allows organizations to concentrate on core human resources functions, while permitting ancillary activities such as benefits administration to be contracted out to a specialist. In-house human resources operations, *as well as other operations,* tend to grow in bureaucratic inefficiency and waste. Nowhere is this more evident than in our federal government. Leaner, outside firms can perform the same operations better, faster, and with fewer resources.

Additionally, many organizations considering downsizing, turn to outside organizations for severance benefit and out-placement assistance. In fact, downsizing is good news for entrepreneurs specializing in these fields.

Temporary And Contract Employee Brokers

Layoffs have created a booming industry for companies that broker temporary and contract employees.

Independent Specialists

Welcome to the age of mass free agency. For hundreds of special tasks, corporations are turning to consultants and independent contractors who specialize in one or a few key processes. Demand for training and development specialists will increase over the next several years. This growth is consistent with an increased emphasis on internal and external customer service and on the need for employees to develop new skills and competencies. Companies are taking a return on investment approach to measuring the effectiveness of training and development initiatives. They realize people are both assets and costs to the organization; the expenditures of time and money are investments that need to show a return.

Companies also are turning to government agencies, graduate students, and retired executives for advice. M.B.A. students, in particular, are accepting aggressive, discipline-related project assignments with local businesses. They essentially are "killing two birds with one stone." They are completing a school project for which they will receive a grade and getting their foot in the door with a potential employer. If the project is a success, both parties emerge victorious. In fact, the frequent use of M.B.A. students on key projects have allowed some large corporations to cut labor costs without resorting to layoffs.

Travel Services

Stressed-out Americans are indulging in affordable luxuries and seeking ways to reward themselves. They are attempting to balance boredom at work with stimulating activities outside the workplace. The failure to cure boredom can result in "I don't care" attitudes, negative emotions and behaviors, psychological withdrawal from work, stress, procrastination, and death-in-life. (Not to mention errors, poor judgment, accidents and injuries, and overall uninspired thinking.) Travel allows one to explore new interests and perspectives, release built-up tensions, and restore one's energy resources. Adventure travel packages are becoming more popular, fueled by the American desire for roads unexplored. With increased expenditures on adventure travel packages, as well as increased business travel expenditures in a globalized economy, travel-related industries face a rosy future.

Technology Too

Americans are attempting to protect themselves from the harsh, unpredictable realities of the outside world. Increasing numbers of workers are abandoning their hectic urban jobs and returning to the more-relaxed pace of small town life. Of those workers who choose to remain in and around big cities, increasing numbers are shutting themselves up inside their homes and filtering out the outside world with sophisticated technologies. These technologies include answering machines, home shopping networks, and virtual-reality fantasy games.

Companies are continuing to automate mundane processes, freeing employees to concentrate on the more creative and personal aspects of service. Perhaps we'll finally witness the much-needed disappearance of the QWERTY keyboard? The QWERTY keyboard, defined by the first six keys in the upper left-hand corner of the traditional keyboard, has been in existence for over 125 years. Since it's been around for so long, it must be the most efficient design in existence? Wrong. The QWERTY keyboard was designed to *slow down* the typist to keep the moving parts from jamming if the typist moved too quickly. Another example of American corporations clinging to past business practices. In case you hadn't noticed, the modern computer doesn't have "parts" capable of jamming. Many modern keyboard designs, such as the Dvorak Simplified Keyboard (DSK), have been proven to increase typing speed and reduce errors, after a brief learning curve. Individuals capable of typing 55 to 60 words per minute accurately on the QWERTY keyboard, often have found it possible to type over 100 words per minute accurately on the DSK.

New insurance products will emerge to offer better protection to the information-based organization. Such products will cover the value of data, information, and media.

As our society becomes more technologically-literate, the acceptance of technology-based sales and marketing will become more widespread. The true value of technology will be in its ability to connect consumers, producers, and suppliers together, eliminating the need for paper and paper shufflers. Yes, it's true technology will put paper shufflers out of work; however, this dislocation will be a short-term one.

New Business Development

Numerous individuals affected by downsizing have formed businesses of their own, often in fields in direct competition with their former employer. Many have formed such corporations out of revenge, but many more have formed such corporations out of the desire to take control of their own destinies. *Ask yourself what would the competitive environment be like if all victims of mass layoffs were to pool their financial and knowledge resources together to form corporations to compete directly with their former employers?* Right now, I'm imagining pools of sweat collecting on the furrowed brows of some of America's top executives. *Downsizing ultimately will intensify the competitive battlefield of the future...employees today, competitors tomorrow.* If you're contemplating a layoff, don't be surprised to discover numerous venture capital firms and other investors are lining up to meet with your soon to be ex-employees. It's the future of new business development. More importantly, if your former employees represent a significant portion of your customer base, what would the competitive environment be like if they all decided to become customers of your chief competitor? What would happen if all former AT&T employee-customers decided to switch their long-distance services to MCI?

CONCEPT IN ACTION

In the summer of 1995, a fifty-five year-old, fully-licensed insurance agent and executive with thirty-one years of insurance industry experience, was released by his employer. Do you think he just rolled over and played dead? Not even close! He used his many years of industry knowledge and wisdom to form his own insurance agency and now has a thriving business of his own. It wasn't easy, but his investment in himself paid off. *The fact is, layoffs often don't signify the end of one's world; they signify new beginnings.*

Career Discovery And Planning

Working men and women, questioning personal and career satisfaction and goals, are opting for simpler living. Our personality types, brain-dominance profiles, learning styles, and values strongly influence our perceptions of the world. This explains why different people are interested in different things, are drawn to different fields, and often find it difficult to communicate with each other. The point is, it is the responsibility of every American to find out who they are and how they can use who we they are to our nation's advantage. George Foster, former major league outfielder, stated it best:

> "What you are is God's gift to you and what you do with what you are is your gift to God."

As a result of the American desire to bring purpose and focus back into their lives, career discovery and planning have become hot-growth industries.

"The way I see it, if you want the rainbow, you gotta put up with the rain."
—Dolly Parton, actress and country-western star

Arthur Miller's *Death of a Salesman* and Myers-Briggs Type Indicator

Key learning from *Death of a Salesman*: *Arthur Miller's* Death of a Salesman *is a story about self-awareness and the tragic consequences of choosing the wrong career path. Both Willy Loman, the drama's main character, and his oldest son, Biff, love working with their hands, and are happiest when they can express themselves through some type of physical labor. The only difference is Biff is aware of this, while Willy is not. Willy's lack of self-awareness contributes to his decision to become a traveling salesman, rather than a carpenter or gardener, and, ultimately, to his suicide. At the funeral, Biff expresses to Willy's neighbor, Charley, "...the man didn't know who he was," and to his younger brother, Happy, "I know who I am kid."*

The first step in career planning, is gathering data on yourself—your abilities, interests, preferred activities, skills, and values. You must learn to see yourself clearly and objectively. Consider how closely your self-image is tied to your occupation, rewards that are important to you, and what makes you happy in work. Various self-assessment instruments are available to assist you in this first step. One such instrument is the Myers-Briggs Type Indicator.

The Myers-Briggs Type Indicator primarily is concerned with the differences in people that result from where they prefer to focus their attention, the way they prefer to acquire information, the way they prefer to make decisions, and the way they prefer to orient themselves toward the outer world. People prefer to focus their attention and energy on the outer world of people and things (*Extroversion*) or the inner world of ideas and impressions (*Introversion*). They prefer to acquire information through their senses (*Sensing*) or through patterns and possibilities (*iNtuition*). People prefer to make decisions based on logic and objective analysis (*Thinking*) or values and subjective evaluation (*Feeling*). Finally, they prefer to take either a planned and organized approach to life (*Judging*) or a flexible and spontaneous approach to life (*Perceptive*). An individual's "type" is the combination of his or her four preferences. For example, an INTP prefers to focus their attention on the inner world of ideas and impressions (I), prefers to acquire information through patterns and possibilities (N), prefers to make decisions based on logic and objective analysis (T), and prefers to take a flexible and spontaneous approach to life (P).

Understanding your personality type can help you choose a career. People tend to be attracted to, and are most satisfied in, careers that provide them with the opportunity to express and use their preferences. For example, those who prefer intuition and thinking may be attracted to, and find satisfaction in, the following careers: computers, engineering, law, management, physical science, research, and technical work.

Remember, Willy Loman loved working with his hands. Thus, if the Myers-Briggs Type Indicator is accurate, Willy preferred sensing and thinking. If only Willy had preferred sensing and *feeling!* Then, and only then, could he have been attracted to, and found satisfaction in, a sales career.

Chapter 5

Downside To Downsizing

"Business must be run at a profit...else it will die. But when anyone tries to run a business solely for profit...then also the business must die, for it no longer has a reason for existence."

—Henry Ford, American automobile manufacturer

Beware Of False Profits

Many organizations downsize to reduce corporate costs, strengthen share price, or take advantage of technological advances, but it has its dangers. First, it can devastate employee morale. Organizations need motivated, productive employees who are ready to accept challenges and to take initiatives. Unfortunately, downsizing efforts typically result in deceptive reports; false optimism; hasty judgments; rumors; and mistakes in communication, decision making, and planning. Second, it can hamper the organization's ability to grow. Eliminating too many employees, or, more importantly, *the wrong employees,* can weaken the organization rather than make it more efficient. After it had announced plans to eliminate tens of thousands of jobs, IBM, for instance, had to contend with lower employee morale and productivity, which led to poor-quality products and services, higher costs, and shrinking market share. Even downsizing cannot save poorly-managed corporations. Thus, companies that undertake internal reorganizations for the sole purpose of increasing profits, in reality, leave a negative imprint on the bottom line. Therefore, the goal of any organization is to create *value,* not profit.

Customers do not buy products and services; they buy value. *In fact, every organization is a value-delivery system.* Thus, one of management's greatest responsibilities is to eliminate or minimize the obstacles to value delivery. Value-delivery obstacles may include, but are not limited to, the following:

- Conflicting demands on the service team's time.
- Fear of trying something new.
- Inadequate levels of authority and responsibility.
- Inadequate work facilities, equipment, and other "tools."
- Lack of ability.
- Lack of bottom-up, as well as top-down, communication flows.
- Lack of a clear understanding of the team's purpose and role.
- Lack of cooperation and support.
- Lack of commitment, effort, and involvement.
- Lack of enthusiasm.
- Lack of mutually-understood goals.
- Lack of training.
- Measuring one thing, reinforcing another.
- Poor leadership.
- Preaching one thing, rewarding another. (You get what you reward regardless of what you preach. If you preach team performance and you reward individual performance, you'll get individual performance every time.)
- Restrictive policies that negatively affect job performance and customer satisfaction.
- Vision without direction. (Visions only inspire when they are expressed in terms of what exactly needs to be done and what is expected of people.)

The key question is *what circumstances exist that are hindering our ability to deliver value to the customer? A key point to consider is, that, in the age of downsizing, the customer isn't at the top of the organization. Nor is the customer at the bottom. The customer is at the center. Essentially, the customer has replaced the middle manager, becoming the heart of the organization.*

The Customer is at the Center of all Organizational Activities

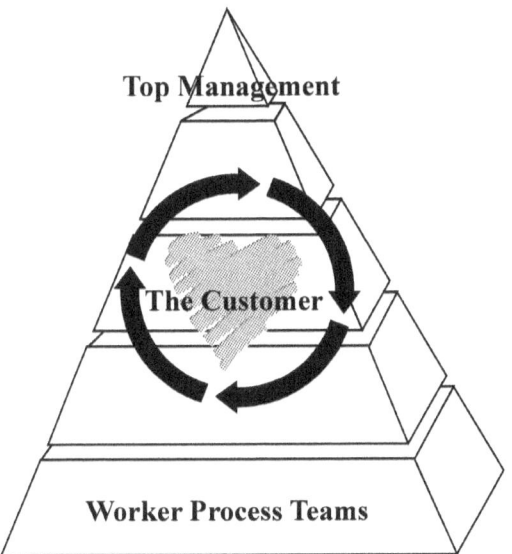

Financial Measurement Systems And Customer Value

An organization's financial measurement system can aid or hinder its ability to deliver value to the customer. If an organization attempts to monitor every possible financial measure under the sun, it runs the risk of spreading its resources too thin. Simply put, the organization is overloaded with data, much of it useless. It can take considerable time and resources to sift through the mountains of data. Thus, managers either ignore the data or spend too much time analyzing it. This can hamper organizational control and decision making, especially if vital information is lost or overlooked. Managers simply do not have the time to take in all the data, decode it, understand it, and act on it. If, on the other hand, an organization attempts to monitor only one or two financial measures, it runs the risk of not having enough information available for planning, spotting problems, or devising solutions in advance. What's worse than having too much or to little information? Having the wrong kinds of information. An organization's financial measurement system must provide timely, complete, and relevant information. Relevant information is aligned with the anticipated business needs and strategic direction of the company. Not every financial measure is appropriate for every organization—an organization's financial measurement system must be designed to support the company's critical success indicators and core business processes.

Although not every financial measure is appropriate for every organization, most companies would do well to begin with basic measures for sales, inventories, and operational expenses. Measures for return on investment, net profit, and cash flow should also be developed. It's also important to measure the organization's working capital needs, net cash cycle, and capital structure. A warning flag report, incorporating these measures, should be developed for sensitive areas of operations, monthly profit and loss statements and budgets for purchases and controllable expenses should be prepared, and break-even points should be monitored. Cash flow is of particular importance. Cash flow shows the inflows and outflows of cash for operating, financing, and investing activities. It is helpful in evaluating the liquidity, financial flexibility, and operating capability of the organization. No matter what measures the organization settles on, each employee must be trained in their interpretation and usage. Such measures will not serve the customer if each employee does not understand them and does not know what to do with the information each measure provides. For instance, you cannot expect an employee to help you improve cash flow if he or she does not understand what the different components of cash flow are and how they are related.

Mass Layoffs Affect Entire Communities

Individuals are not the only ones who must face the financial and psychological obstacles of mass layoffs. Entire communities are affected by subsequent declines in individual and corporate tax revenues, retail sales, and single-family home values; declines in the quality of education as teachers are laid off; increases in alcoholism, gambling, and suicide; increases in crime as police officers are laid off; and increases in taxes to support the growing unemployment and welfare roles. Additionally, the infrastructure disintegrates as construction jobs disappear and maintenance crews are laid off. Spend just one week in a former industrial powerhouse like Joliet, Illinois or Gary, Indiana, and you'll know exactly what I mean. What's even darker, some corporations are using the threat of mass layoffs and the resulting financial and psychological obstacles as leverage to secure credit, real estate, regulatory, and tax breaks.

Technology-Driven Changes

New technologies have contributed to downsizing. First, new technologies contribute to downsizing as industrial and service jobs are lost to artificial intelligence, expert systems, and smart robotics. Second, while wireless hookups are giving employees more discretion to live and work where they please, such technologies are allowing employers to shift their workplaces quickly, often devastating or uprooting entire communities. Third, new technologies have resulted in the de-skilling of American workers. For instance, laser scanning devices have de-skilled the job of the grocery store checkout clerk. Such jobs involve less pay and prestige and have helped reduce American wages toward a global average. Wouldn't it make more sense to attempt to raise global wages toward the American average? The answer to this vital question depends on whether you believe in lifting the people of the world up or tearing Americans down.

CONCEPT IN ACTION

Unlike the competition, Mr. Pasteur's Ice Cream Factory[*] outlets are company-owned. Louis Koch, Chief Executive Officer, views franchising as a loss of control over the end product and loss of touch with the customer. The organization is relatively flat, with few levels of authority. The number of employees reporting to each manager varies throughout the hierarchy, but in general is broad. This broad span of control allows the field sales staff to respond more quickly to customer needs and keeps management focused on solving business problems rather than on managing layers of people.

Pasteur's is loosely structured, with no official organization chart. Thus, the informal organization plays a major role in communications. The loose organizational structure allows communications to take place between people as needed, regardless of title or position.

Pasteur's top management needs some control over the decentralized decision-making hierarchy. Thus, the company invests heavily in strategic-information technology to manage programs pro-actively. Information systems provide informational support for decisions throughout the hierarchy.

Power accrues to functions that are considered to be the most important to organizational effectiveness and survival. Thus, the size of Pasteur's Management Information Systems (MIS) staff has continued to increase to coordinate the blossoming of technological activities in four areas: financial, operations, sales, and store-level systems. Power accrues to the "information gatekeepers" within the MIS department. An information gatekeeper derives his or her power from the authority to plan, organize, and control the flow of information resources to achieve organizational goals.

Mr. Koch has automated mundane processes, freeing people to concentrate on the more creative and personal aspects of service. The sophisticated store-level management information system helps the organization manage key business processes, including accounting and inventory control, electronic mail, employee scheduling, marketing support, production planning, sales projections, and skill testing to encourage learning and self-development. This "expert system" is designed not only to automate the routine elements of the activities, but also to learn how to respond to exceptions by prompting the manager for input each time an exception is encountered. As the system and the manager learn, the exceptions become routine. The system forces the manager to use critical thinking skills to determine how the current situation is *like* others they have encountered so they appropriately may apply past knowledge and experience. It also requires the manager to determine how the situation is *different* from others they have encountered so they can identify what must be learned to succeed. Store managers can follow or disregard any recommendations. Unfortunately, many managers may carry out the recommendations without asking whether they make sense to the customer. At Pasteur's, the managers tell an "expert system" what the problem is, review its ideas and suggestions, and then make the decision. This does not allow for initiative, experimentation, and growth opportunities for lower-level employees.

Louis Koch sees information systems as a way to accommodate growth without expanding staff. Besides a cultural fit, individuals are selected for what they bring to the MIS team. The MIS Director consistently encourages the people working with the technology to think up new, creative applications and stimulates innovation by asking team members to learn new skills, try new approaches, or think or act in a different way. They question ideas from many points of view and are motivated to challenge traditional ways of doing things.

Information technology plays two roles at Pasteur's. First, *the system provides control.* The information system helps Mr. Koch maintain a degree of personal involvement with each store manager. Second, *the system provides better decision making.* Each manager must be able to collect relevant data and organize, interpret, and use this data for strategic success. Mr. Koch feels that special problems that need to be solved often are hidden among the numbers. Mr. Koch provides the information technology people need to do their jobs and to make accurate decisions. The information technology also helps managers to link their decisions with the anticipated business needs and strategic direction of the company.

Even though Mr. Koch provides the information technology managers need to do their jobs, voluntary turnover is high. Why is this the case? Perhaps the "expert systems" are too efficient. Perhaps they automate parts of the job the manager really enjoys and would much rather perform without the aid of sophisticated information technologies. The extensive use of information technology at Pasteur's could be undercutting store manager satisfaction, involvement, and commitment.

*Pasteur's is a fictitious corporation developed to illustrate a key point. This case provides an excellent example of how sophisticated information technologies inadvertently can de-skill and de-motivate an entire workforce.

"These are the times that try men's souls."
—Thomas Paine, English-born American Revolutionary patriot and author of *Common Sense*

Plato's *The Republic* and Mary Parker Follett's Principle of Constructive Conflict

Key learning from *The Republic:* *In* The Republic, *Plato, a disciple of Socrates, engages in Socratic dialectic—the practice of examining ideas and opinions using the method of question and answer—with numerous Athenian and Greek philosophers, to identify and solve problems.* The Republic, *written in dialogue form, exposes different ideas and opinions for examination from multiple viewpoints, resulting in enhanced communication and understanding.*

Should leaders resolve conflict or should they stimulate it? Given the potentially-disruptive effects of conflict, leaders need to be sensitive to how it can be managed. Conflict needs to be resolved when it causes major disruptions in the organization and absorbs time and effort that could be used more productively; however, leaders also should worry about the absence of conflict. An absence of conflict may indicate the organization is stagnant and employees are content with the status quo. It also may suggest that work groups are not motivated to challenge traditional and well-accepted ideas.

Although the natural reaction to conflict is to consider it a bad thing, American sociologist Mary Parker Follet insists this is the one thing a leader must not do. In fact, her Principle of Constructive Conflict calls for leaders to stimulate conflict to challenge the underlying assumptions and values associated with alternative solutions. This sometimes is referred to as "dialectical inquiry"—the creation and constructive use of conflict by a leader. Its purpose is to bring about situations where differences of opinion are exposed for examination by all. If, for example, competing organizations are making significant changes in markets, products, or technology, it may be time for a leader to stimulate creativity and innovation by challenging the status quo. Stimulating conflict may provide employees with the motivation and opportunity to reveal differences of opinion that they previously had kept to themselves. When all parties to the conflict are interested enough in an issue to be somewhat antagonistic toward other groups, they often expose their hidden doubts or opinions. In turn, this allows the parties to get to the heart of the matter and, often, to develop unique solutions to a problem. Indeed, the interactions may cause the group to acknowledge there is a problem. Constructive conflict, then, can be a catalyst for creativity and change in the organization.

There are several methods available for stimulating constructive conflict. These include altering the physical location of groups to stimulate more interaction, forcing more resource sharing, and other changes in relationships among groups. In addition, training programs can be used to increase employee awareness of potential problems in group decision making and interaction. Adopting the role of "devil's advocate" in discussion sessions is another method of stimulating constructive conflict between groups. In this role, a leader challenges the prevailing consensus to be sure all alternatives have been considered.

Chapter 6

Never Outsource High Value-adding Business Processes

"Entrepreneurs…understand that you cannot climb the ladder of success without first getting on the ladder."

—Michael Bauman, Professor of Theology and Culture,
Hillsdale College

Know When And What To Outsource

Outsourcing is a common approach to increasing productivity or reducing operating costs; however, it is not enough to outsource functions just to increase productivity or to reduce operating costs. Numerous other factors should be considered when deciding to outsource a particular function: the company's competitive position, critical human resource concerns and the means for addressing them, workforce skill mix and structure, and, most importantly, the value added to the organization by the function in question. Careful study must be made in order to determine those functions that can be outsourced and those that should be done in-house. The point is, corporations must maintain a policy of selective outsourcing.

It's important for today's corporations to specialize in what they do best, that is, to focus on their core capabilities. In their McKinsey Award-winning *Harvard Business Review* article, "The Core Competence of the Corporation," professors Gary Hamel (London Business School) and

C.K. Prahalad (Graduate School of Business Administration, University of Michigan) presented a strong case for focusing on core competencies. In the current business environment of global competition, rapid technological change, and uncertainty, organizations must measure the contribution of employees and functions to the goals of the organization. High-value added employees and functions must be retained. Low-value added employees and functions can be outsourced. Non-value added employees and functions should not be retained.

Identify And Organize Around What You Do Best Or What You Must Do Best

A. Establish a clear and commonly-understood purpose and identify the major lines of business and strategic activities the organization will develop to fulfill its purpose, as well as the critical success factors of the industry

Management must provide organizational members with a shared view of the future, a clear sense of direction, a mobilization of energy, and a sense of being engaged in something important. All organizational members must understand what is important to the company's success and what proficiencies they need to contribute to that success. Begin by asking *what should we know or be able to do to give our company a distinct competitive advantage?* Have organizational members think about the things the organization does well. What contribution do they make to their customers that no one else can do as well? What is the most important thing for the organization to focus on in the future? What purpose do you want the organization to serve and what do you want the organization to become? Should we focus on our access to superior resources, low-cost production capabilities, methods of distribution, operations capabilities, a particular market niche, product quality, technology and constant innovation, or total customer satisfaction?

FOCUS	CORE COMPETENCY REQUIRED
methods of distribution	*Multiple-vendor, multiple-product alliances*: required for superior flexibility in distribution composition mix
a particular market niche	*Ability to find, understand, and capture a unique category or niche*: required to offer peerless product and service value to a targeted customer
technology and constant innovation	*Fast cycle time of development*: required to innovate, sprint ahead of the competition, and respond to competitor offerings, including potential product and service substitutes
total customer satisfaction	*Create value through precise needs assessment*: required to customize solutions based on superior customer knowledge

Identifying sources of competitive advantage helps the organization focus its energies and resources on what's important to the company's success and provides a critical rallying-point for organizational members; however, sources of competitive advantage do not mean anything if they're not marketable. You may be the most-innovative buggy-whip manufacturer in the world, but who cares? Such businesses make a critical mistake when they perceive themselves as producing products or services rather than satisfying customer needs. There are numerous examples of what McKinsey Award-winning professor Theodore Levitt (Harvard University) refers to as "myopic" (nearsighted) corporate behavior. Levitt identifies the failure of the railroads to see themselves as being in the *transportation* business as the critical reason for their rapid decline. Marketing myopia attacked the railroads because they failed to ask themselves "What business are we *really* in?" The ability to anticipate customer needs comes as a result of good strategic exploration and encourages companies to define their purpose in terms of these needs. Other examples of marketing myopia include the U.S. Postal Service and overnight delivery; ABC, CBS, NBC and cable television; IBM and the personal computer.

Some organizations do not suffer from marketing myopia, but rather they suffer from marketing hyperopia (farsightedness). Marketing hyperopia attacks those who are so focused on the future and the long-term purpose of the organization, they overlook the near-term, incremental changes in the industry, in legislation, in a competitor's strategy, or in a customer's behavior that potentially could derail the organization's vision or purpose. It is important for an organization to develop a good balance between short-term and long-term time horizons.

Organizations also must identify their industry's critical success factors, the things a firm must concentrate on doing well just to survive. Critical success factors never should be outsourced since competitive advantage can be built by concentrating on one or several critical success factors and performing them in a manner that is superior to rivals. When is a certain expertise a source of significant competitive advantage? Again, when it matters to the customer.

B. Identify the core processes necessary to accomplish your purpose and establish the critical success indicators the organization will use to track its progress

Identify the core processes by which the organization will achieve its vision of the ideal future state. Organize around the core processes necessary to yield your product or service offering to your customers using multi-functional teams. Never organize around functions. The historical performance of functional organizations is dismal at best—slow response times, conflicts over organizational priorities and resources, and function-specific political agendas. In such organizations, intense value-destroying rivalries between different functions—research and development and manufacturing, for example—are common. Instead, establish management-worker process teams, give these teams specific performance goals, and offer information, training, and other support, including gain-sharing benefits, if possible. Discuss your vision of the ideal future state, and the processes and strategies necessary to achieve it, with the teams to gain alignment and commitment. Process teams are becoming the basic building block of the modern corporation. Corporations are organizing around processes to enhance responsiveness to changing customer needs and to enhance problem-solving capabilities; however, for such action to take place on the front line, employees require a clear understanding about what the organization is trying to achieve. High energy and excitement are products of an environment in which employees are clear about their purposes, the results to be achieved, and their abilities to influence the results. They understand what their key tasks are, and know how their own efforts support the key tasks of the team as a whole. Employees cannot perform if they do not know what the goals of the organization are or how well or poorly they are doing in relation to those goals.

C. Overhaul the organization's culture and structure to support the achievement of the organization's purpose

Too many American corporations simply copy the best practice of another organization without considering how the practice will "fit" with the organization's existing cultural and structural constraints. Organizations must either adapt the best practice to fit these constraints, or break the constraints to fit the best practice.

What is culture? *Culture is the unique pattern of assumptions, behaviors, beliefs, and values a group develops as it learns to cope with and make sense of significant internal and external events.* Since an organization's culture develops as it learns to cope with and make sense of significant internal and external events, is it any wonder American corporations are experiencing a virtual cultural revolution?

An organization's culture is a powerful tool for change. First, and foremost, it establishes the criteria for the allocation of rewards and status and for the recruitment, selection, promotion, retirement, and dismissal of employees. It dictates appropriate and inappropriate reactions to crises. It defines what the organization chooses to emphasize, measure, and attempt to control. An organization's culture can be discerned from the design of physical space; formal statements of organizational creeds and philosophy; legends, myths, and stories about significant events and people; organizational systems and procedures; and the organization's structure. Successfully change any of the above elements, and you change the assumptions, behaviors, beliefs, and values of the entire organization.

An organization's structure impacts its ability to plan, organize, and control the flow of information resources to achieve organizational goals. A narrow span of control with many levels of authority often inhibits prompt response to customer needs and reduces individual freedom and initiative. Simply put, top management is further away from key information sources. In such organizations, the informal organization plays a major role in the management of information. The informal organization evolves to compensate for the coordination problems between functional or divisional groups. In addition to the typical lateral integrating functions—liaison roles, task forces, committees, and teams—information technology can be used to break down barriers among functions or divisions resulting in less response time and quicker decisions.

A relatively flat organization with few levels of authority and a broad span of control allows the organization's staff to respond more quickly to customer needs and keeps management focused on solving problems rather than on managing layers of people. Simply put, top management is closer to key information sources.

Henry David Thoreau's *Walden* and Clemmer's 'Focus' and 'Context'

Key learning from *Walden:* *In* Walden, *Thoreau conveys his desire "...to live deep and suck out all the marrow of life..." and to develop a "Spartan simplicity of life and elevation of purpose." (In my opinion, Thoreau is recommending that we create a single purpose for our lives, or our organizations, and dedicate all available resources to fulfilling that purpose.) The following passage from the pages of* Walden *says it all:*

> *"I went to the woods because I wished to live deliberately, to front only the essential facts of life, and see if I could not learn what it had to teach, and not, when I came to die, discover that I had not lived."*

According to Jim Clemmer, author of *Pathways to Performance*, **Focus** and **Context** are *critical to continual improvement and high performance.* Focus and Context define who you are, who you want to be, and where you want to go.

A major movement in the Western world today is the search for meaning. We want more than just a job or an existence. We want to make a difference. We want to know that our short time on this earth counted for something. We want more than to just exist or get by, we want to live. We want to be energized. We want passion, excitement, and a sense of deeper purpose.

People want meaningful work in an organization with an exciting purpose. What they get is a job. In most organizations, management has created a sterile and passionless culture. Their strategies, budgets, and business plans are cold and lifeless. So teams and frontline performers go through the motions, put in their time, and go home.

Effective leaders [create focus and harness] the deep urge we all have to be part of something meaningful...They transform jobs into crusades, exciting adventures, or deeper missions.

[They discuss, debate, and decide] on the answers to these three questions: Where are you going (your vision or picture of your *preferred future*)? What do you believe in (your *principles* or values)? Why do you exist (your *purpose* or niche)? Clemmer calls these the Three Ps. They are critically important questions. They're fundamental to leading yourself and others. This is the beginning point of effective leadership. These basic issues are the fabric with which you weave your Focus and Context. If you're attempting to change your team or organization culture, your answers to these basic questions define the culture you're trying to create.

(From *Pathways to Performance* by Jim Clemmer, copyright ©1995 by The Clemmer Group, Inc. Used by permission of Prima Publishing, a division of Random House, Inc., and Jim Clemmer, president of The Clemmer Group, Inc., Kitchener, Ontario, Canada. Full text available at www.clemmer.net.)

Identifying Your Core Processes Means Identifying Your Core Customers

The key to success is to focus on your sources of competitive advantage. To begin, identify who your most profitable customers are, discover what they value, then dedicate all your resources on delivering value to your most profitable customers. Since you cannot be all things to all people, doesn't it make sense to concentrate on being all things to your most profitable customers only? Doesn't it make sense to concentrate on the customers who are making you money? The classic Pareto Principle supports the fact that you make eighty percent of your profits from only twenty percent of your customers. Identify the twenty percent, what they value, and deliver value to them! *Stop over-serving your low-value clients!* This requires the development of demographic, behavioral, and purchase preference profiles for the twenty percent. Such information can be used for two purposes. First, the information can be used to combine the elements of product, price, promotion, and place into a superior value package. With this superior value package you can influence customer behavior and maximize profit contribution. Second, the information can be used to identify and target prospects with similar profiles indicating high profit potential. In past decades, many companies diversified into totally unrelated industries, attempting to be all things to all people. Although the industries looked promising, the companies lacked the appropriate skills and knowledge to compete. A prime example is Sears' venture into retail financial services.

CONCEPT IN ACTION*

Retail financial services encompass all financial products and services aimed at the consumer market (general public). Financial and non-financial firms alike have attempted to develop retail financial networks to offer consumers "one-stop" financial shopping. These financial conglomerates provide insurance, savings and investment products, real estate, and other financial services to consumers.

Retail financial services gained strength in the volatile economic environment of the 1970s. Rising inflation and interest rates forced consumers to seek higher returns. This factor, in turn, forced financial institutions to develop alternatives to traditional financial products and distribution systems. Experimentation with new products and systems intensified with deregulation.

Financial conglomerates make sense only if the lines of business are related. For example, non-financial firms should not sell financial products and services. First, the competitive environments of each line of business are too diverse. This diversity often forces management to spread resources too thin. In addition, it draws management attention away from the firm's core business units and reason for existence. However, non-financial firms should be encouraged to engage in joint ventures with established financial firms to develop innovative credit-extension plans for their core customers.

Second, the consumer purchasing process for a financial product differs in intensity and duration from the consumer purchasing process for a non-financial product. For example, it is unlikely any consumer will analyze a new mutual fund with the same mind set as they would a new pair of shoes.

Even purely financial institutions often find it difficult to mix and match financial lines of business. For example, banking institutions may find it difficult to market insurance products. The regulatory environments of each line of business are too diverse and the competition too intense. The bank would have to hire additional management expertise to help the firm navigate the multiple regulatory environments. In addition, management would have to stretch the firm's resources to compete on multiple fronts.

An insurance company, on the other hand, may find it relatively easy to market mutual funds. The regulatory environments and the competition for each line of business are similar. In fact, the insurance industry created annuities to compete with the growing mutual fund market.

Most importantly, sophisticated consumers demand individual attention and customized service. Thus, consumers often make financial transactions and plans with multiple, specialist firms. For example, they purchase their life insurance from a life insurance company and they purchase their securities from an unrelated brokerage service. This point is important since most consumers are reluctant to "place all their eggs in one basket."

Four factors made financial services attractive to Sears in the early 1980s. First, demand for innovative financial products and services was growing rapidly as Sears' customer base became more sophisticated. Second, Sears was not affected by restrictive banking industry regulations and other barriers to entry. Third, Sears believed it could capitalize on its experience with financial products gained through its credit card operations. Fourth, Sears had extensive retail experience.

This retail experience had enabled Sears to establish a national distribution network, to understand the needs of its customer base, to secure the trust of Middle America, and to develop a vast pool of financial resources and information technologies. Each strength is a prerequisite for success in the financial services industry. Unfortunately, Sears' position of strength had diminished significantly from a peak in 1969.

First, Sears' store environment did not provide a suitable atmosphere for discussing insurance, real estate, and other financial transactions. Whereas it is likely customers will buy shoes and *socks* on the same shopping trip, it is unlikely customers will buy shoes and *stocks* on the same shopping trip. Second, whereas Sears understood the needs of its customer base, the retail giant was slow to meet those needs. This provided smaller, faster-moving competitors an opportunity to gain market share. Third, inconsistent retailing practices were eroding Middle America's trust in Sears. Fourth, and most important, Sears' existing distribution networks were poorly managed with weak cost controls. Mismanagement of the Sears distribution system ultimately was responsible for the firm's weakened financial position. This indicated Sears may not have the financial resources to meet the capital needs of a growing financial network. Thus, Sears' strengths did not support diversification into financial services.

The Sears Financial Network, as a whole, provided an earnings boost to the declining retail giant from 1982 to 1991. For example, the core merchandising business, accounted for 55% of total revenues in 1991 (down from 70% in 1982). The total asset turnover ratio for the core merchandising business was 1.27 (down from 1.36 in 1982). This ratio indicates that for every $1.00 in assets, the core merchandising business generated $1.27 in sales. The core merchandising business accounted for 38% of corporate net income (down from 50% in 1982).

The financial network, on the other hand, accounted for 45% of total revenues in 1991 (up from 30% in 1982). Unfortunately, the growing financial network required large amounts of assets to produce sales. The financial network's total asset turnover ratio was .33 in 1991 (down from .44 in 1982). This ratio indicates that for every $1.00 in assets, the financial network only generated $.33 in sales. Fortunately, the financial network was well managed with strong cost controls. Thus, the network provided 62% of corporate net income (up from 50% in 1982).

Each business segment of Sears, Roebuck & Company grew from 1982 to 1991, with the majority of the revenue and profit growth coming from the financial network. The results for each segment are as follows:

RESULTS FROM 1982 TO 1991
REVENUE GROWTH PROFIT GROWTH

	REVENUE GROWTH	PROFIT GROWTH
ALLSTATE	159%	52%
COLDWELL BANKER	243%	17%
DEAN WITTER	209%	12%
SEARS MERCHANDISING	52%	12%

The results from 1985 to 1991 were less impressive with two segments, Coldwell Banker and Sears Merchandising, showing declining profitability:

RESULTS FROM 1985 TO 1991
REVENUE GROWTH PROFIT GROWTH

	REVENUE GROWTH	PROFIT GROWTH
ALLSTATE	112%	21%
COLDWELL BANKER	30%	(38%)
DEAN WITTER	126%	345%+
SEARS MERCHANDISING	18%	(37%)^

SPECIAL NOTES:

+From 1985 until 1987 the Discover Card lost about $400 million before taxes, all borne by Dean Witter. The Discover Card became profitable in 1988. Sears envisioned the Discover Card as the key to the financial network.

^Sears' declining profitability resulted from increased competition and a higher cost structure than the competition. During the same time period, for example, Wal-Mart's revenues grew 419% and profits grew 392%. In addition, Wal-Mart's total asset turnover was 2.84 in 1991.

In late 1992, Sears abandoned its grand plan to meet both the merchandising and financial-services needs of middle-income Americans. On a positive note, this decision will enable Sears to reduce its debt burden and to re-focus its strategic orientation back on its core merchandising operations. On a negative note, Sears is retaining its under-performing merchandising operations while divesting the more-profitable financial operations. Thus, in the future, Sears' struggling merchandising operations will have to move forward without the support of the financial network.

There are many reasons for the decision to divest the non-core financial services network. First, management actions to shore up the struggling merchandising operations were failing. Second, restructuring plans were not well-received by Wall Street. In fact, relentless pressure from stockholder activists, particularly Robert Monks, to break up the company to maximize investor value, was perhaps the primary reason for the move. Before the move, Sears' stock significantly was under-performing the market; after the move, Sears' stock went up 3 7/8, adding more than $1 billion in value. Third, Moody's lowered Sears' credit rating. Fourth, the growing financial network required capital resources the merchandising operation didn't have and couldn't get.

Sears' decision to divest its financial services network is in their shareholders' best interests. The lines of business simply were not compatible. After all, diversification into the financial services industry forced management to spread resources too thin. In addition, it drew management attention away from the firm's core merchandising operations and its reason for existence. These two factors, in combination, provided smaller, more-focused competitors an opportunity to gain market share. Most importantly, synergies did not develop between the various parts of the financial network, as sophisticated consumers continued to make financial transactions and plans with multiple firms. Several other organizations, including financial institutions, have found it necessary to divest unrelated financial units for this reason.

*The financial figures used in this case were taken directly from public financial records, including 10-K filings. This case is one of the most widely-studied cases in modern MBA programs. It's important to note that since spinning off periphery businesses and focusing on its core merchandising operations, Sears has experienced double-digit increases in income growth and steadily-rising sales per square foot.

"I have learned this, at least, by my experiment: that if one advances confidently in the direction of his dreams, and endeavors to live the life which he has imagined, he will meet with a success unexpected in common hours."

—Henry David Thoreau, American transcendentalist essayist, naturalist, and author of *Walden*

Chapter 7

To Thine Own Self Be True

"Destiny is no matter of chance. It is a matter of choice: It is not a thing to be waited for, it is a thing to be achieved."

—*William Jennings Bryan, American statesman and orator*

More than 40 million jobs were eliminated between 1979 and 1999 as a result of corporate downsizing. Millions more are trapped in un-satisfying careers, unable to advance within their companies or move to another. Is it any wonder job security and career satisfaction rank number one and two, respectively, on the list of concerns of middle-income Americans?

Don't Sit Back And Wait For It To Happen To You: Manage Your Own Job And Career Security

You have a choice. You can sit on your butt and hope your company doesn't strip you of your security blanket. Or, you can get off your butt and manage your career within your company or manage your career move to another company. The odds of losing your job (one in ten) are far greater than the odds of winning a pick-six/forty-seven number lottery (one in 10,737,573); yet, millions of Americans are more likely to invest in the lottery than they are in their own career development. Is it any wonder middle-income Americans are falling far short of fulfilling their dreams?

With promises of job security and career ladders gone, the emphasis has shifted from "employment" to "employability." All employees must learn to manage their own careers and develop the skills and competencies necessary for long-term career success. It is important to note that about half of all American corporations will be in knowledge-based industries by the year 2000. Thus, a starting point for career development will be in learning to collect, organize, interpret, and use information to make decisions and to solve problems. If you do not thrive (or cannot learn to thrive) on creative and innovative applications of computers, software, and information technologies, your career is in jeopardy. What's more important, if your company doesn't provide you the opportunity to increase these skills through training and education and keep you informed of growth opportunities throughout the organization, get out *now* and find one that does. You have another choice to make as well. You can work for an organization served by a culture that is held together by rigid work rules and regulations. Or, you can work for an organization served by a culture that is held together by a commitment to creativity, freedom, initiative, and innovation. *Never allow any organization to control your destiny. Never leave your job or career security to chance. Take control of your life and live your dreams. If you don't, someone else will. Your future does not exist; it is created by your actions (or lack thereof).*

Think Small

Do not overlook small businesses for career opportunities. As job opportunities disappear at the nation's largest businesses, small businesses are hiring, providing job growth and energy to keep the economy going. Remember, with a large business, you're a little fish in a big pond. If you make a mistake, you can hide it. Unfortunately, the flip side is if you make an incredible contribution to the corporation, it's often hidden as well.

Not only that, in today's world, you can do everything right, and still lose your job. With a small business, you're a big fish in a little pond. If you make a mistake, you can't hide it. Fortunately, the flip side is if you make an incredible contribution to the corporation, it's visible as well. With a small business, you're given the opportunity to create the future, stretch your skills, and show the world what you're made of. I know you've been told since you were old enough to wear pants, to think big. Don't. Think small.

Put Your Career Through A Workout To Enhance Your Employability

- Be bold and courageous in everything you do, and every so often, push your luck. Reputations are made by searching for things that cannot be done and doing them.

- Commit yourself to constant improvement. Stretch your capabilities every day to learn new skills in your profession and industry. More importantly, develop cross-functional, non-industry-specific skill sets to keep you prepared for professional or industry-specific downturns that could impact your job security.

- If you don't enjoy your job, find a new one. Before it's all said and done, you will spend three-quarters of your life at work. Do you want to remain in a job that isn't enjoyable or doesn't provide you with a sense of purpose? Work that isn't enjoyable and doesn't provide a sense of purpose does not contribute to career satisfaction or to organizational effectiveness.

- A corollary to the previous point, get off your butt and do something that's enjoyable and provides a sense of purpose! The greatest waste of our natural resources is the number of people who never achieve their potential and never fulfill their dreams.

- Keep a positive attitude and demonstrate enthusiasm. Nobody wants to hire or work with a perpetually-pessimistic human being.

- Learn to listen; opportunity often knocks very softly. Continuously look for the opportunities that surround change.

- Learn to master the "inner game" to perform well in the "outer game." Use positive mental affirmations and visual reminders to release the power of both the conscious and subconscious minds to achieve goals. Never allow a negative word to become your master.

- Monitor your results and chart your progress, making adjustments in your approach whenever necessary. Update your resume often and keep fresh copies readily accessible.

- Network to get your foot in the door. Begin with friends and acquaintances and build your network from there.

- Write a personal mission statement that provides you with an empowering, ennobling, fulfilling, inspiring, and uplifting purpose and vision for your life. After all, workers who have a sense of purpose are motivated, enthusiastic, and energetic and provide better service to customers. Engage in basic goal setting and put a workable action plan in place.

Six Skills For A More Secure Future

1. Communication Skills

American businesses require workers who are able to listen intently and question effectively to gain information and to understand opposing points of view. You must be able to locate, obtain, and organize information from both human and electronic sources; to present and defend views through formal and informal, written and oral, presentations; and to provide the information people need to do their jobs and to make accurate decisions.

2. Interpersonal Skills—Leadership

American businesses require workers who are able to build a positive, productive work environment. You must be able to articulate shared ideas, goals, and visions and organize effort to achieve goals; to measure performance in relation to goals and provide timely feedback and rewards to others; to tailor reward systems to match individual desires, hopes, plans, and problems; to provide challenging and stretching tasks and assignments to motivate and develop entire units or organizations; to encourage prudent risk taking to overcome unproductive and/or restrictive biases, rules, and traditions; to hold staff responsible and accountable for decisions; and to manage conflict through open dialog and candid discussions.

3. Technology Skills

American businesses require workers who are able to access electronic information libraries, corporate data banks, and other information sources. You must be able to use knowledge of personal computers and spreadsheet, database management, and statistical software to convert relevant data into useful information.

4. Problem-Solving Skills

American businesses require workers who are able to identify and define problems. You must be able to use information to aid problem solving; to use abstract reasoning to propose and evaluate solutions; to allocate and marshal resources to put solutions and strategies in place; and to know how strategies and tactics will play in the marketplace.

5. Multi-Cultural Skills

American businesses require workers who are able to develop a global perspective. You must be able to maintain openness to different ideas and various points of view and to accept diversity in others.

6. Creative/Innovative Skills

American businesses require workers who are not afraid to embrace avant-garde concepts, ideas, and strategies even when they go against conventional wisdom. You must be able to create structured chaos to encourage personality and originality of vision, and to stimulate inventive genius; to bring the creative ideas of others to the marketplace; to go out of beaten paths and to have adventure with the unknown; to accept change and uncertainty as challenges; to tackle challenges with high energy, drive, and optimism; to see the possibilities and to create opportunities; to adjust to new conditions and situations; and to assume prudent risks and learn from both successes and failures.

Identify your strengths and weaknesses on each of the above competencies. Then commit yourself to additional training, informational interviewing, and self-initiated research projects. More importantly, select learning activities designed to enhance your existing strengths and to reduce or eliminate your existing weaknesses. Some example learning activities are included below.

Example Learning Activities

A. Communication Skills

Develop an audience profile for a communication or training endeavor to identify who they are, what their problems are, and what they need. In addition, define the purpose for the endeavor and analyze whether you accomplish the purpose. Develop visually-memorable media that underscores key points, creates understanding, and ignites action. Since you can listen faster than anyone can talk, use this rate difference to your advantage by trying to stay on the right track and thinking back over what the speaker just said. Encourage everyone to participate in a group discussion by directing questions to the ones holding back. When you are impressed with a remark or insight offered by another, say so. Do not allow anyone to "put down" another because that person has a different point of view.

B. **Interpersonal Skills—Leadership**

Compare and contrast what it means to be a manger and what it means to be a leader. Find an initiative, lead, and ask team members to identify strengths and weaknesses in your leadership style. Identify people who get things done and model their behavior. Confidently assign projects designed to stretch the abilities of your employees. Expect them to be successful, but do not expect them to be perfect. Design a program to have team leadership responsibilities earned, re-earned, and rotated. Point out the connection between the work others do and the goals of the organization.

C. **Technology Skills**

Take one or several computerized reports or other information packages that cross your desk and trace where they originate and where they go. Take one or several reports or packages and look at who uses them, how they can be combined, how they can be made more effective, more timely, and more relevant at a human interaction point—that is, when somebody meets an internal or external customer. Anticipate the impact of emerging technologies and widely-distributed information on your work, power, and influence. Take additional information technology courses and apply what you learn immediately.

D. Problem-Solving Skills

Engage in bold "what if?" exercises and let your mind wander to what it would really take, by others you count on and yourself, for your biggest problems to go away forever. Scale your thinking so the magnitude of the solution matches the size and persistence of the problem. Anticipate the impact of your solutions, answers, and results on the goals of the organization. Describe your solutions, answers, and results to others to see if you anticipated accurately. Invite others to help you analyze and solve problems.

E. Multi-Cultural Skills

Draw an organization chart that represents the skills and reporting relationships needed to win against world-class competitors in the emerging global marketplace. Compare and contrast the chart with your current organization chart. Develop an understanding of how the workforce is changing with numbers, demographic composition, knowledge, and values. Value other people's weaknesses, actions, and differences. Respond to people's feelings as much as to their ideas.

F. Creative/Innovative Skills

Stimulate innovation by asking team members to learn new skills, try new approaches, or think or act in a different way and monitor their response to change. Read books on scientific theories and discoveries and brainstorm potential real-world applications.

Industry Situation Analyses Aren't Just For Organizations Anymore

Organizations engage in industry situation analyses to assess an industry's long-term growth potential. Some industries are full of opportunity and growth potential, while others are stagnant or in decline. Such analyses, in combination with competitive situation and company situation analyses, help an organization address strategic issues and problems. Typically, industries that are full of opportunity and growth potential drive up the demand for labor; industries that are stagnant or in decline drive down the demand for labor. In other words, *an industry's long-term growth potential ultimately determines an industry's long-term employment potential.* Thus, each individual employee must engage in industry situation analyses to answer the question *is this an attractive industry to be in?* If you decide not to seek employment in another industry, your enhanced understanding of your industry, your competition, and your company will make you more valuable to your current organization and its customers. If you decide to seek employment in another industry, your enhanced understanding of that industry will leave you well ahead of the competition. The point is, in the age of downsizing, you must be prepared.

Chapter Theme Song: "*Give to Live,*" **Sammy Hagar**

Plutarch's *Biography of Fabius* and Modern SWOT Analysis

Key learning from *Biography of Fabius:* *Plutarch's* Biography of Fabius *describes the conquests of the Roman General, Quintus Fabius Maximus, who is best known for his defeat of the Carthaginian General, Hannibal, in the Second Punic War. His unpopular strategy to delay confrontation with Hannibal earned him the nickname "The Cuncator" or "The Delayer" from his fellow Romans. Fabius "…thought it not seasonable*

---

to engage with the enemy…" since "…the Carthaginians were…in want of money and supplies…" Ultimately, Fabius knew his enemy (competitor) and knew himself; his decision to delay confrontation worked—Hannibal, unable to supply his troops, was forced to return to Carthage. (In my opinion, Plutarch's Biography of Fabius *is the Western equivalent of Sun Tzu's* The Art of War *introduced in Chapter 8; however, Sun Tzu takes the concept of "know the enemy and know yourself" to levels unimagined by either Plutarch or Fabius.)*

Situation analysis typically includes a search for SWOT—*strengths, weaknesses, opportunities,* and *threats*—that affect organizational performance.

Internal strengths and weaknesses: Strengths are positive internal characteristics the organization can exploit to achieve its strategic performance goals. Weaknesses are internal characteristics that may inhibit or restrict the organization's performance. The information sought by leaders to evaluate strengths and weaknesses typically pertains to specific functions such as finance, marketing, production, and research and development. Internal analysis also examines human resource characteristics, management competence and quality, and overall organization structure. On the basis of their understanding of these areas, leaders can determine their strengths and weaknesses relative to their competitors.

External opportunities and threats: Threats are characteristics of the external environment that may prevent the organization from achieving its strategic goals. Opportunities are characteristics of the external environment that have the potential to help the organization achieve or exceed its strategic goals. Leaders evaluate the external environment with information about the task environment and the general environment. The task environment sectors are the most relevant to strategic behavior and include the behavior of competitors, customers, and suppliers. The general environment sectors have an indirect influence on the organization and include economic conditions, legal/political events, socio-cultural changes, and technological developments. Additional areas that might reveal opportunities or threats include interest and pressure groups and potentially-competitive industries.

Chapter 8

Public Serpents: The Government Is Part Of The Problem

"Government isn't the solution: it's the problem."

—Ronald Reagan, fortieth President of the United States

Clinton's Tax Policy Is 'Crazy'

The inside cover of Van Halen's compact disc "5150," shows Michael Anthony, Sammy Hagar, Alex Van Halen, and Edward Van Halen in straight jackets. The CD's title comes from the last four digits of a mental hospital's phone number. "5150" is a symbol for "insanity, lunacy, craziness." Bill Clinton's massive tax hike passed the Senate 51-50. How ironic!

If history is any guide, higher personal and corporate income taxes now will contribute to bigger deficits, higher unemployment, rising inflation, and failed local school district tax levies and bond issues over the long run.

Bill Clinton's "deficit-reduction plan" will produce bigger deficits over the long run for two reasons. First, personal and corporate income tax increases dampen economic activity and reduce the revenue base. Consequently, Clinton has overestimated the revenue gains from the tax increases. This largely is because Clinton's estimates fail to take into account the extent to which people alter their behavior to keep their tax burdens as low as possible. *Americans do not want to work harder or to take risks just to pay higher taxes.*

Let's look at what happened in November and December of 1992. Those expecting increased taxes in 1993 accelerated income in 1992 and deferred deductions until 1993. It's not just the wealthy: those expecting lower taxes in 1993 deferred income until 1993 and accelerated deductions in 1992. In addition, tax-deferred and tax-free investments are more popular than ever.

Second, the forecast of higher tax revenues encourages more government spending. The Democrats are too fast to raise taxes and too slow to cut spending. The bulk of deficit reduction must come from cuts in social spending and defense outlays. When the government does spend, the money should go toward education, infrastructure, science and technology, and training for displaced workers—the items necessary for this country to compete.

Higher tax rates also will contribute to higher unemployment over the long run by absorbing funds that otherwise would be channeled into the expansion of existing businesses and the creation of new ones. As a result, fewer job opportunities will be created.

Higher tax rates also will contribute to rising inflation over the long run as the wage-payer passes the tax increase on to the consumer, who pays it in the form of higher prices for goods and services.

Higher tax rates also will contribute to failed local school district tax levies and bond issues over the long run by absorbing funds local residents otherwise would have available to channel into local school systems. It's not that local residents do not want strong school systems they can be proud of. They do. Unfortunately, with higher federal tax rates, they have little, if any, income left to invest at the local level.

As John Henry Boetcker said: "You cannot help the wage-earner by pulling down the wage-payer. You cannot help the poor by destroying the rich."

The American Dream?

Broken families and tax payer-supported abortions, convoluted rules and regulations, crime and drugs, the elderly and the poor, racial and class conflict, swelling unemployment and welfare burdens, the young and the hopeless...*Is this to be the American legacy?*

The Democrats do not want to dismantle any of the programs put in place by Franklin D. Roosevelt, our thirty-second president, to pull the United States out of the depths of the Great Depression. Many Democrats see the longevity and continued existence of his Depression-era programs as their memorial to him. I wonder how FDR would feel if he knew the Democrats' memorial to him is bankrupting our nation, both economically and morally? His welfare programs, strengthened by our thirty-sixth president, Lyndon B. Johnson, and his so-called "Great Society" programs, have fostered a culture of dependency, perpetuating the poverty they were designed to end. The traditional American values of family, opportunity, responsibility, and work have been replaced with government, victimization, dependency, and entitlement. Even FDR admitted his welfare programs were meant to be temporary safety nets, not lifetime support systems. *Perhaps it's time to pull the plug?*

America's welfare system rewards undesirable behavior. For example, numerous alcoholics and drug addicts receive Supplemental Security Income "disability" checks that they use to purchase more alcohol and drugs. In many cases, alcoholism and drug addiction have become tax payer-supported habits. This is not to say that SSI does not serve a useful purpose in our society; it does, but only when it benefits the truly disabled.

America's anti-investment, anti-savings, anti-success, anti-work tax code has reduced your opportunity to pursue the American Dream. *I ask you, if our current tax system is designed to "soak the rich," why is the middle class drowning?* Direct taxes are the single-largest expense in your family's budget. Nearly forty percent of your income is siphoned off by the government through direct taxation. *Are you getting your money's worth?* Before you answer this question, consider the additional hidden costs of excessive government regulations and frivolous litigation passed on to the consumer in the form of higher prices for goods and services. Again, before you answer this question, consider the impact of increased payroll taxes on your family. As payroll taxes are increased by the government, corporations are responding by downsizing their payrolls. Add to this your share of the national debt and you have little, if any, income left to invest in a business, a new home, or your children's education.

America's educational system is failing, especially in math and science. Sure, we crank out more chemists, electrical engineers, environmental scientists, materials scientists, microbiologists, optics researchers, and physicists than any other nation in the world. Unfortunately, most are foreign born and return home shortly after completing their studies. Students from Asia, especially the 'Asian Tigers'—Hong Kong, Japan, Korea, Singapore, and Taiwan—are flooding American universities. The fact is, it's easier for them to do it than it is for native-born Americans. *No matter what you've been told, such nations do not beat us with "cheap" labor; they beat us with "skilled" labor.* Ira Magaziner, management consultant and presidential advisor, stated it best:

> "Over half our trade deficit comes from foreign industries
> that pay their workers higher wages than we do."

To make matters worse, Japanese scientists and executives religiously attend academic conferences in the United States and meticulously study and translate research papers. Others tour American factories, laboratories, and plants to glean the best ideas and make them their own. How many American scientists and executives do the same?

To make matters even worse, cash-strapped university labs have turned to the Asian Tigers for much-needed funding. The Japanese, in particular, are not afraid to invest in basic research that may not pay off for many years. This gives Japan immediate access to the world's best and brightest engineers, mathematicians, and scientists. At this juncture, it's important to note that American universities have produced more Nobel Prize winners than any other nation. These individuals just want to create and discover—and they're loyal to whoever gives them the opportunity (as well as the capital) to solve nature's deepest mysteries and to venture into uncharted territory. Perhaps that's why W. Edwards Deming, "Father of the Third Industrial Revolution" and a top leader in statistical quality control, took his ideas to Japan at General Douglas MacArthur's request? Deming has had such an incredible impact on Japan's economy, the Japanese have named the most honored quality award in Japan after him: The Deming Prize. What does Japan get in return for its investment in basic research conducted by America's best and brightest? Sole patents on the research conducted. The evidence is overwhelming: when America's best and brightest cannot find adequate capital at home, they sell out to foreign entities, denying their own nation of the potential earnings for capital, repeating the vicious cycle. Americans invented the computer, the facsimile machine, the micro-wave oven, the television, the video-cassette recorder, the oil drilling and refining equipment in use throughout the entire Middle East, and almost every form of modern communication equipment available, just to name a few. How many of these inventions are manufactured by American corporations today?

Budget deficits, coupled with an anemic national savings rate and private over- consumption, pass the cost of government programs onto the next generation. *This means we do not pay for our own mistakes. Therefore, we do not learn from them.* America's debt is eroding our ability to save, invest, and compete in the global marketplace. Non-competitiveness often translates into lost jobs and rising unemployment. Additionally, deficit spending raises interest rates and increases the cost of borrowing. As a result, the Asian Tigers can raise capital much more cheaply than can American firms. American firms must pay five times what their Japanese rivals pay to raise capital. This means American firms only can afford to invest in new products or technologies with quick payoffs—three years or less. The Japanese, on the other hand, can afford to invest in new products or technologies that will not payoff for decades.

Other Forces Contributing To Downsizing

There now is a trend toward downgradings by insurance rating agencies, putting pressure on companies to shed their poorly performing businesses and develop adequate capital to support the growth of their remaining businesses. Much of the insurance industry is basing current and future strategy on the false hope of continued regulatory protection; the insurance industry is spending far more in lobbying efforts to guard protected status than in preparing for inevitable competition inherent in an open market. *Ignoring the reality of a changing marketplace, including alternative distribution channels such as the Internet, is dangerous.* IBM's downfall clearly should indicate that no company can ignore the realities of a changing marketplace and prosper. Consumer preferences and behavior are driving the evolution of the marketplace. Exposure to delivery alternatives and increases in consumer sophistication and familiarity with technology clearly is accelerating.

Labor union contracts often impose restrictive staffing practices or other work rules that artificially diminish productivity within union firms. Such restrictive practices and rules have accelerated the substitution of capital for labor and hastened the search for cost-reducing, productivity-increasing technologies. That is to say, when faced with higher production costs due to union demands, employers are forced to reduce costs and improve production techniques that use less labor per unit of output. In short, labor unions have contributed to technological progress and downsizing.

In July 1993, IBM announced it would lay off 60,000 employees. This announcement was enough to add thirty percent to the value of IBM's stock by year end. Additionally, IBM's chief executive officer was paid $15.2 million for the year, roughly 157 times the average IBMer's pay. It was discovered that Robert Allen, AT&Ts Chief Executive Officer, after announcing plans to dismiss 28,000 employees, had been awarded $25 million in compensation for the year. That translates into over $890,000 for every employee dismissed! *What's wrong with this picture?*

"I can feel the value of my stock options
increasing already..."

Layoffs, and rumors of layoffs, are popular since they bring quick results. Wall Street is quick to abandon a company at the first sign of softness in quarterly earnings. Compounding that pressure, many companies have to contend with raiders, takeover artists, and other "paper entrepreneurs"—individuals who simply shuffle existing wealth around rather than create new wealth. As you can see, American managers are under pressure from stockholders and owners to produce high monthly and quarterly results. As a result, short-term employee performance is the only thing that's monitored and rewarded. Rewards should encourage long-term, not short-term, thinking; the compensation system should be tied to the long-term performance and profitability of the company.

In short, we borrow more than we save, consume more than we produce, import more than we export, spend more money than we earn, and redistribute wealth rather than create it. If the words of John F. Kennedy are on target, we are on our way to second-class status.

"An economy hampered with restrictive tax rates will never produce enough revenue to balance the budget, just as it will never produce enough jobs."
—John Fitzgerald Kennedy, thirty-fifth President of the United States

Sun Tzu's *The Art of War* and Competitive Intelligence

Key learning from The Art of War:
—*"Therefore I say, 'Know the enemy and know yourself'; in a hundred battles you will never be in peril."*
—*"When employing troops it is essential to know beforehand the conditions of the terrain."*
—*"All warfare is based on deception."*

Around 500 BC, the great Chinese military strategist, Sun Tzu, wrote a treatise on *The Art of War*. This work is as relevant today as it was 2,500 years ago. (In my opinion, *The Art of War* is the Eastern equivalent of Plutarch's *Biography of Fabius* introduced in Chapter 7; however, Sun Tzu takes the concept of "know the enemy and know yourself" to levels unimagined by either Plutarch or Fabius.) *The Art of War's* main theme is powerful, yet simple: foreknowledge (intelligence **collection**) and deception (intelligence **protection** or counterintelligence) are the keys to success. To prosper in today's global economy, you must know your enemy (competition), know yourself (your own company), and know your terrain (marketplace); additionally, you must make it difficult, if not impossible, for your enemy to know you. This especially is important on foreign soil where the terrain is less familiar, the rules of engagement are different, and the competition has the home-field advantage.

The business environment is a giant jigsaw puzzle of highly-fragmented data, much of it useless. This is where competitive intelligence, or CI, comes into play. The purpose of CI is to make sense of the business environment by identifying and fitting the relevant data pieces together to form as complete a picture as possible. Some of the pieces will be missing, and a few will not fit perfectly, but if done effectively, CI can yield a pretty decent model of the actual business environment in which your company operates. With its roots in government and military intelligence, CI can enable you to

- Identify competitor capabilities (what he can do) and intentions (what he plans to do)
- Check capabilities and intentions against competitor actions (what he actually does)
- Discover new or potential competitors
- Identify competitor strengths and weaknesses
- Identify competitor blindspots and vulnerabilities (where he can be attacked)
- Identify competitor strongholds (where the risk of attack is too great)
- Anticipate competitor reactions to your strategic moves
- Learn from the successes and failures of others
- Develop personality, psychological, and decision-making profiles of rival firms' executives
- Estimate market or industry growth rates and potential
- Identify the key success requirements of the market or industry
- Identify and segment target markets
- Identify market opportunities or threats
- Construct future industry scenarios
- Assess the key operating capabilities, critical processes, and core competencies of your company
- Measure your company's performance, identify where performance improvement is needed, and make performance improvement recommendations

- Identify your company's strengths and weaknesses
- Identify your company's blindspots and vulnerabilities (where you can be attacked)
- Examine the potential impact of emerging technologies on your competitor, your company, and your market
- Benchmark actual business practices, methods, and costs of your competitors
- Examine potential merger and acquisition candidates and alliance or joint venture partners
- Participate in the strategic planning process, generating and evaluating alternatives and making recommendations as to the best strategy in light of external environmental factors
- Monitor consumption outlook, plant expansions or closures, or signs of changes in financial condition of major customers
- Anticipate future product and service needs of existing customers and discover new or potential customers (opportunities for new business)
- Advise senior management on advertising, sales promotion, and PR campaigns; distribution channel management; new product and service development; and program pricing

In case you think "competitive intelligence" is the same as "espionage" or "spying," think again. Talented CI professionals DO NOT resort to misrepresentation, trespass, or wiretapping. All the data they need to complete the picture is publicly available, published, or can be collected from human sources, much of it from internal company experts. In fact, according to Faye Brill, Chief Information Officer of Ryder System, "Eighty percent of what you need to know is inside your company." Keep in mind, it is perfectly legal to "figure out" another's "trade secrets" if all the collection methods used to acquire the information are themselves legal. It's also important to note that legal standards differ from country to country; what's "illegal" or "unacceptable" in the United States—bribery, for example—might be considered "legal" or "acceptable" in another country. Primary CI data sources include:

- Case studies;
- Commercial databases, clipping services, directories, and electronic search services;
- Commissions, including building, business development, commerce, economic development, planning, trade, and zoning;
- Company visits/correspondence;
- Competitor speeches and public statements, including press releases;
- External experts including consultants, customers, financial analysts, securities analysts, and suppliers;
- Financial reports including annual reports and credit reports;
- Help-wanted ads;
- Industry associations, conferences, seminars, and trade shows;
- Industry or market surveys;
- Internal company experts including customer service, government affairs, human resources, marketing, procurement, public affairs, and sales;
- Libraries;
- Product brochures;
- Public disclosures including 10Ks and regulatory filings;
- Published materials including books, newspapers, and trade magazines;

- Uniform Commercial Code (UCC) filings; and
- Websites.

What role does "counterintelligence" play in this process? Keep in mind as you attempt to "know your enemy," your enemy is attempting to "know you." Therefore, it is important to put reasonable protections and counter-measures in place to safeguard your trade secrets against disclosure. Reasonable protections range from eliminating noncompliance information from public filings to shredding discarded documents, including envelopes. Employee education, training, and awareness programs also are important since inadvertent disclosures often occur during the course of day-to-day human interactions. An overzealous sales representative may, for example, disclose a little tantalizing tidbit of information to make the difficult sale. Or, an employee may disclose confidential information during a job interview with a prospective employer to demonstrate their expertise or value to the firm. All it takes is for a carelessly-misplaced communication—electronic, hard copy, or verbal—to fall into enemy hands, and your business plans or strategies will be exposed.

Finally, as in war, it often is necessary to employ "chaff" to misdirect or confuse the enemy so they will be unable to respond effectively when the time comes. *Your enemy must never know where or when you plan to attack.* Here is just one example. When asked by the press about a possible new product launch, give answers that leave open many possibilities. (Or, don't respond at all—silence can be a very powerful ally.) If your competitor makes it known they expect you to launch the new product in Seattle, and you do not plan to do so, do not correct them. Afterall, they came to the conclusion on their own. Instead, let them waste valuable resources in Seattle preparing for an attack that will never come. You may even hold a new product launch press conference in Seattle to reinforce the enemy's erroneous conclusion. Then when you launch the product in Columbus, they enemy will be completely unprepared.

Chapter 9

Public Servants: The Government Can Be Part Of The Solution

"It is not the strongest of the species that survive, nor the most intelligent, but the one most responsive to change."

—*Charles Darwin, British naturalist and originator of the theory of evolution*

Why not a permanent capital-gains tax credit?

The needs of our economy for capital investment during the next few years cannot be overemphasized. If the challenges of greatly increased foreign competition are to be met, and if domestic problems are to be solved, a tax structure must be developed that will encourage corporations and individuals to accumulate and invest capital.

Republicans and Democrats both recognize the importance of incentives for capital investment to create jobs and promote economic growth and productivity; however, neither party can reach agreement on how to achieve this goal. The Republicans prefer a permanent capital-gains tax cut; the Democrats prefer a temporary investment tax credit.

The solution is simple: combine the two ideas into a permanent capital-gains tax credit. With a permanent capital-gains tax credit, the capital gain will be exempt from any taxation if the *entire* gain is invested in land, buildings, or fixed assets (production equipment or pollution control facilities) within twelve months before or after sale.

In addition, the capital gain will be exempt from any taxation if the *entire* gain is invested in research and development, education and training, and health and safety within twelve months before or after sale. If the entire gain is not invested within twelve months before or after sale, the entire capital gain will be taxable at ordinary income-tax rates.

We need to encourage corporations and individuals to accumulate and invest capital. The capital-gains tax credit will offer all Americans the benefits of a productive and more competitive economy.

The Government Has The Potential To Unleash The Job-Creation Machine

The key to long-term prosperity is how quickly America can transform the results of corporate restructuring and technological advances into a job-creation machine. America has the potential to create new industries, new jobs, and new products that can compete effectively in global markets. Isolationism and protectionism aren't the answers. Among America's greatest assets is our free-market system, which provides the opportunity for the constant creation of new enterprises and new jobs. We must begin by investing in the development of America's West Coast. America's West Coast constitutes a major part of the rapidly-developing Pacific Rim. For the United States to play a pivotal role in its development, we must invest in education, infrastructure, science and technology, and training for displaced workers.

We need to encourage the development of high-tech regions similar to California's Silicon Valley and Boston's Route 128. We need to discover why cities like Cincinnati, OH-KY-IN; Las Vegas, NV; Orlando, FL; Phoenix-Mesa, AZ; Raleigh-Durham-Chapel Hill, NC; Seattle-Bellevue-Everett, WA; and Tampa-St. Petersburg-Clearwater, FL are thriving while cities such as Joliet, Illinois and Gary, Indiana are struggling to survive. In search of an answer, I looked over numerous publications on what a city like Raleigh-Durham-Chapel Hill, voted "The Best City for Business" by *Fortune* in 1993 and "The Best Place to Live in America" by *Money* in 1994, has to offer and found the following: abundant or quick access to natural resources, including labor; access to competitive financial resources; commercial space (hotel, industrial, office, retail); convention, exhibit, and meeting facilities; highly-educated population; low crime rate; medical and health-care facilities; reasonable tax burdens and relatively low cost of living; recreation, tourism, and cultural amenities; sound infrastructures, including communications (magazine, newspaper, radio, telephone, television), transportation (air, rail, road, waterways); utilities (electricity, natural gas, sewerage, solid waste disposal and recycling, water); and world-class colleges and universities, including Duke, NC State, and UNC-Chapel Hill. Is it any wonder Raleigh-Durham-Chapel Hill is ranked among America's best enterprise- and job-creation markets?

Reinventing Government: A Checklist For Positive Change

√Adopt conservative fiscal management policies. Slash our debt and discard Keynesian Economic Theories that support deficit spending and drain our nation of value. By borrowing to cover its own deficits, the government competes with private enterprise for precious capital. This reduces the amount of capital available for new plant and equipment and research and development. A smaller deficit will reduce interest rates and lower the cost of borrowing. This will lead to faster growth, which, in turn, will produce a net increase in government revenues.

√Change outmoded accounting standards. Inventory buildup is the most common cause of economic cycles. The economic booms and busts we blindly have come to take for granted as a necessary evil in a free-market economy must be eliminated. Most organizations, including real estate development corporations, build up inventory levels to buffer the organization against uncertainty. In addition, traditional cost accounting standards treat inventory as an asset. In reality, inventory is not an asset when you take into account the carrying costs (the cost of deterioration and obsolescence, insurance costs, the opportunity cost of tying up funds in inventory that could be used elsewhere, and storage costs) associated with it. The point is, inventory is just as much a liability as it is an asset.

√Cut foreign aid and invest in America first. Why should we place foreigners above Americans? We must teach foreign nations they must depend on themselves and not on "American welfare." America must take a return on investment approach to all foreign aid. Each time we invest abroad, we should ask ourselves *are we getting our money's worth?*

√Develop a new "Made in USA" labeling system. Require 98% domestic content of both *parts and labor* to secure the "Made in USA" label. Allow the labels "Made in USA by an American Corporation" and "Made in USA by a Japanese (or some other foreign) Corporation" to be included on any product meeting the new domestic content standards. Prohibit American corporations who manufacture products in foreign nations, from marketing the products back home as "American made." The products may be owned by an American corporation, but they're certainly not American made.

√Elect competent leaders who add value to our society.

William Shakespeare's *King Lear* and William Sandy's Leadership Selection Criteria

Key learning from *King Lear:* *If you can get past the point that leaders were not "selected" during Shakespeare's time, but arose to power through hereditary succession,* King Lear *is a story about leadership selection and the tragic consequences of selecting the wrong leader. To drive this point home, Shakespeare develops a distinct double plot: The fates of King Lear, a mythical pre-Christian king of Britain, and his daughters (Goneril, Regan, and Cordelia) are paralleled by the fates of the Earl of Gloucester and his sons (Edgar and Edmund). Both Lear and Gloucester suffer from "filial ingratitude" and a fatal lack of insight, resulting in deceptive reports; false optimism; hasty judgments; rumors; and mistakes in communication, decision making, and planning. The notion of "sight" or "vision" as an important leadership trait is reinforced frequently throughout the drama; for example,*

> *King Lear: "Out of my sight!"*
> *Earl of Kent: "See better, Lear…"*

According to William Sandy, performance improvement consultant and author of *Forging the Productivity Partnership*, there are several criteria or characteristics that are critical in selecting leaders. Pick a leader who:

- Brings sense to the mission
- Can build a team, figure out precisely what diverse contributors bring to the end result, and get the best out of them
- Can give pinpointed counsel to strengthen output
- Has high standards; cares about what happens

- Is a good communicator, both for clarity of direction and to get people excited
- Is credible and consistent; will earn the right to be listened to
- Is willing to innovate and take measured risks to achieve breakthroughs
- Is willing to listen
- Is willing to measure what happens, take the heat and responsibility, and keep the focus on results rather than sideshows
- Sees the possibilities of change
- Understands the role of communication to help people understand
- Understands the role of knowledge to help people grow
- Understands the targeted audience and cares about their problems
- Will patiently earn receptivity for new ideas; coach, teach, and lead by example; and make adjustments when required
- Will share credit; will build upon other people's foundations, including the work of predecessors

(Sandy, William. **Forging the Productivity Partnership**. New York, NY: McGraw-Hill, 1990. Used with permission of The McGraw-Hill Companies.)

√Encourage American labor unions to organize labor in foreign nations, especially in Mexico. The critics of the North American Free-Trade Agreement (NAFTA) argue that cheap Mexican labor will create "a giant sucking sound" as American corporations head south. American labor unions would benefit by discarding this line of thinking and entering Mexico to organize their labor. The benefits of such an effort would be two-fold. First, America would benefit since these efforts should slow the downward movement of American wages toward a global average and quicken the upward movement of foreign wages toward the American average. Second, unions would benefit since these efforts would reverse decades of declining union membership.

√End world dependence on Middle-Eastern oil. Begin by uncapping the numerous closed oil fields in America's heartland, creating jobs for Americans and revenues for America. Next, form an oil consortium with other non-OPEC nations, including Russia, Norway, Mexico, China, the United Kingdom, Canada, and Brazil to compete directly with OPEC for world oil revenues. Lastly, encourage joint ventures between American automobile manufacturers and American oil producers to develop, manufacture, and mass market super fuel-efficient automobiles, as well as, *commercially-viable alternative-fuel automobiles*. Encouragement can be provided in the form of a *joint venture research and development incentive*.

√Fortify the nation's infrastructure. Invest in communications, transportation, and utilities, especially in high-tech regions. Repeat the successes of Silicon Valley and Raleigh-Durham-Chapel Hill throughout the United States. Additionally, we must begin to build roads to last using high-tech materials and production technologies. If we build roads to last, we can spend less on routine maintenance and repairs and more on improvements and new projects to keep pace with economic growth and changing transportation patterns.

√Foster partnerships between American businesses and university laboratories, between science and industry. As the Japanese have proven, the industries of the future do not always emerge in response to market forces. Give American corporations first crack at the basic research (and the resulting patents) conducted in university laboratories. Boost funding for science and technical education of native-born Americans. Require foreign-born products of American universities to put in at least two years with an American corporation before returning home.

√Make all pensions and health-care programs portable.

√Make the government adhere to the same accounting principles and standards it imposes on American corporations.

√Overhaul the guidelines for immigration to America. At the turn of the century, we got highly-skilled immigrants from Europe; now we get un-skilled immigrants from Asia and Latin America. America no longer can afford to accept and support the world's huddled masses. If it can be proven the individual can add value to our society, then and only then, should he or she be given the opportunity to pursue the American Dream. Additionally, deport all criminal aliens and make all non-citizens ineligible for welfare and other government programs. Finally, tear down the fence between America and Mexico and dig a canal instead. For a cost far smaller than that of providing welfare and other government benefits to illegal immigrants, the American-Mexican border can be closed permanently. The benefits of such an effort would be five-fold. First, it would slow the flow of illegal immigrants across America's border. Second, unemployed American and Mexican labor could be employed to construct the canal. Third, the canal, connecting the Gulf of Mexico with the Pacific Ocean, would present the opportunity for inland states to take advantage of Pacific Rim developments. Fourth, it would reduce the world's reliance on the Panama Canal. Fifth, profits from the canal's operation would give a much-needed boost to the American and Mexican economies.

√Place a cap on the amount of restructuring charges a corporation can take against income in a single year. This should serve to reduce unnecessary corporate restructurings. Additionally, limit the amount of interest payments on debt burdens resulting from leveraged buy-outs that can be deducted from taxes in a single year. This should serve to curtail leveraged buy-outs and reduce business debt.

√Put an end to America's unilateral free-trade policies. If the Japanese are going to put up barriers to American investment in Japan, we should put up barriers to Japanese investment in America. This isn't "protectionism," it's good economic sense. We allow Japanese corporations to come in and acquire leading-edge American corporations on our open market,

while any American attempt to acquire leading-edge Japanese corporations soundly is defeated. If Japan puts legislation in place to restrict
American ownership of Japanese corporations, we should put legislation
in place to restrict Japanese ownership of American corporations.
Additionally, we allow Japanese corporations to sell to their full potential
in America, while any American attempt to do the same in Japan soundly
is defeated. If Japan puts legislation in place to restrict the number of
automobiles General Motors (or Chrysler or Ford, for that matter) can sell
each year in Japan, we should legislate the same restrictions against
Honda, Nissan, and Toyota in America. I'm not suggesting we should
blame Japan for our problems; we only have ourselves to blame. We presented Japan the opportunity to buy us out without any reciprocity and
they did exactly that. I'm also not suggesting America should abandon its
free-trade policies altogether; we should practice total free-trade only with
nations who practice it with us. Also, I'm not suggesting Japan is the only
nation taking advantage of our unilateral free-trade policies; in fact,
European countries, including the United Kingdom and Germany, own
far more of America than Japan does.

√Put an end to life-time appointments to the Supreme Court. Amend
the U.S. Constitution to place term limits on Supreme Court justices. We
must send a clear message that justices serve only to *interpret* the law, not
to *make* the law.

√Reduce barriers to new enterprise and stimulate entrepreneurial
initiative by altering the tax code. Our tax code must reward entrepre-
neurship, risk taking, saving for the future, and work. We must promote
business investment by allowing businesses to claim tax deductions as
investments in equipment and research and development are made rather
than writing them off gradually over several years. (Yes, depreciation is
another outmoded American accounting practice.) Additionally, scrap all
ideas for either a permanent capital-gains tax cut or a temporary investment
tax credit; instead, enact the *permanent capital-gains tax credit* introduced
at the beginning of this chapter. Finally, increase the average propensity to

save and invest relative to the average propensity to consume, while simultaneously keeping inflation and unemployment in check. This can be accomplished by cutting income taxes, lowering interest rates, increasing consumption taxes, and forming government/business partnerships to expand exports relative to imports.

√Reduce the regulatory bureaucracy and put an end to frivolous lawsuits. It doesn't make sense to saddle our corporations with oppressive regulations and frivolous lawsuits, especially when the same burdens do not affect our foreign competitors. The costs of excessive regulations are not borne by the corporation anyway, but rather they are borne by the consumer, in the form of higher prices for goods and services.

√Reinvent government by privatizing operations and downsizing. Privatize federal assets and services, including federal loan programs, public housing, Amtrak, and the Tennessee Valley Authority, to name just but a few. Terminate unnecessary federal programs, as well as, incompetent, inefficient, or slothful employees. Do not be afraid to adapt the three-step value-delivery process revealed in the chapter on high-value added processes: establish a clear and commonly-understood purpose and identify the major lines of government and strategic activities the government will develop to fulfill its purpose, as well as the critical success factors; identify the core processes necessary to accomplish the government's purpose and establish the critical success indicators the government will use to track its progress; and overhaul the government's culture and structure to support the achievement of the government's purpose. You might want to keep in mind the overall purpose of government, like any institution, is to provide value to its customers. (Or, in the case of government, its employer. Think about that one for a moment.)

√Require foreign corporations doing business in America to pay the same tax rates and to comply with the same regulations as American corporations.

√Shift welfare funding into jobs programs, requiring work for benefits. Again, deny non-citizens welfare benefits. Do not provide any additional payments for additional children, or mandate the use of birth control among welfare recipients. I know this sounds harsh, but if American taxpayers are going to foot the bill, they have the right to dictate lifestyle choices. Afterall, it's their money. The "rule of one and two" should be applied to welfare participation: once a life and for two years only. It should be a program to help people get back on their feet, not a lifetime support system. Please keep in mind, it doesn't take a village, just strong family values.

√Upgrade public education and establish a national apprentice program to replace vocational training. America's failure to invest in human capital has damaged our ability to compete. Too many American workers lack the skills necessary to perform today's knowledge-intensive jobs. To begin, establish a national course of study: English language and literature (reading and writing); mathematics; science and technology; social studies, including history and geography; art, music, or another discipline designed to stimulate creativity and lateral thinking; personal and household finance; and commercially-viable foreign languages. Yes, the English language should be made the official language of America; however, all Americans should be required to learn to read and write at least one commercially-viable foreign language in the course of his or her primary education. In Germany and Japan, students are required to read and write in their native tongues as well as in English. To remain competitive in the global economy, students in America should be required to do the same. I hope you took special note of my recommendation for mandatory 'personal and household finance' coursework. It should be obvious by this point in the game that our most powerful ally in the battle to reduce mounting consumer debt is education. We teach our students how to read, write, multiply, and divide, but we do not teach them how to manage their money, credit, and investments—what a wasted opportunity! Good conduct also should be taught, shaped by in-school discipline, if necessary. Students arrested for violent crimes or for the possession of drugs or weapons immediately should be removed from the traditional school setting and enrolled in special military-style academies for the duration of their primary education. It's time to start rewarding students who exercise good conduct and punishing those who don't; students who exercise good conduct should be given the opportunity to learn in an environment free of fear. Dropping out from high school also must be discouraged. This can be accomplished by denying high-school drop-outs welfare and other government benefits, including the right to drive a car. Those who complete high school and decide not to go on to college, should be required to enroll in a national apprentice program for two to four years of schooling together with on-the-job training sponsored by local corporations. Under such a program, graduates would receive a technical certificate along with a school guarantee for technical competency. Finally, shift power from the administrators and unions to the parents and local corporations. To compete in a global economy, we must repeat the successes of Thomas Jefferson High School for Science and Technology in Alexandria, Virginia throughout the United States. Additionally, we must repeat the successes of Jaime Escalante, an immigrant math teacher in a tough, inner-city high school in Los Angeles and subject of the hit movie *Stand and Deliver*, throughout the United States.

American Values

It's been said that Americans have no shared national culture to unite them as the Japanese have. Baloney! Americans can succeed by returning to their roots. American values that served us well in the past, can provide us a source of competitive advantage now and in the future: accomplishment; entrepreneurialism, invention, and rugged individualism (tempered with a return to basic family and community values); freedom and initiative; optimism and opportunity; results-orientation; risk taking; a sense of destiny, direction, and discovery; and spontaneity.

Chapter Theme Song: "*Raise a Little Hell,*" Trooper

*　　　　　*　　　　　*

ACTION ALERT!

Your Representative Needs to Hear from You!

See an idea you like in Chapter 9?

Call, write, or e-mail your representative today and let them know you saw the idea in Christopher M. England's *Outsourcing the American Dream*!

(Or better yet, buy them a copy of this book and mail it to them with your favorite idea highlighted!)

General Addresses:

The President
The White House
1600 Pennsylvania Avenue NW
Washington, DC 20500

The Honorable _____
United States House of Representatives
Washington, DC 20515

The Honorable _____
United States Senate
Washington, DC 20510

(NOTE: More specific addresses can be found in the various Congressional directories available at your local library, or on-line. Check out http://www.house.gov/writerep for a sophisticated on-line repository of mailing addresses, phone numbers, and e-mail addresses.)

Chapter 10

American Leadership In Action:
Customer SATURNfaction

"To be a success in business, be daring, be first, be different."

—*Marchant*

The Saturn Project was initiated in 1982 as a small car project for General Motors. Its goal was to manufacture, market, and service a car that could beat the Japanese in the small car arena. Since its incorporation in 1985, Saturn has changed everything…manufacturing…marketing…service. Saturn has become a symbol of quality in American manufacturing and an industry standard by which almost every other automobile manufacturer, domestic or foreign, must measure its ability to serve its customers.

Saturn has proven itself best-in-class in the highly-regarded J.D. Power and Associates New Car Customer Satisfaction Index and New Car Sales Satisfaction Index studies. In 1995, Saturn finished among the industry elite in the Customer Satisfaction Index, ranking third behind only Lexus and Infiniti, putting Saturn in a class with luxury cars whose prices begin at three times that of Saturn. The Customer Satisfaction Index is based on product quality and dealer service after one year of ownership. In 1995, Saturn ranked first in the Sales Satisfaction Index. Once again, Saturn proved you don't have to pay luxury-car prices to receive world-class service. The Sales Satisfaction Index is based on the customer's buying experience and the sales staff's skills.

Value-Oriented Culture

Saturn has created a culture based on *involvement, commitment,* and *quality.* Saturn realizes that employees want to be involved in decisions that affect them. Involvement helps employees to better understand and serve the business and the customer. This involvement, in turn, spawns commitment and a deep sense of ownership. Finally, this sense of ownership helps Saturn pursue the highest quality standards in the automobile industry.

From its inception, Saturn has tried to be different. Saturn executives feel that much of the American automobile industry has been operating poorly for years. Their goal has been to change the traditionally-negative image of the American automobile industry, especially at the dealer level. Saturn is attempting to accomplish this through a fanatical devotion to quality and customer satisfaction. Other entities with chronic image problems, including the federal government, the insurance and legal professions, and auto mechanic and repair shops, could learn much from Saturn's efforts.

Saturn's world-class manufacturing strategy was made possible through the historic agreement reached in July of 1985 between *General Motors* and the *United Auto Workers.* The agreement cleared the way for unprecedented teamwork between GM and the UAW. Saturn's *Customer Action Council* brings people from different functional areas, including engineering, marketing, production, sales, and service, together for decision making and problem solving. Select members of the Strategic Action Council also participate in the process. This arrangement enables Saturn to integrate the CAC's recommendations directly with the strategic planning process. Information systems incorporating business, communications, parts, sales, and service databases also are used to aid decision making.

Saturn uses its dealership service bays and its voluntary recall programs to reinforce the image of Saturn as a company dedicated to quality and total customer satisfaction. Service bays are located in the front of the building, rather than the back, to "keep customer problems up front" rather than delegating them to some secretive, back-room process. In August of 1993, Saturn voluntarily notified all owners of 1991-1993 cars (350,000 plus vehicles) of the campaign to replace the generator wiring harness with a new, safer design to eliminate the *potential* for an engine fire due to *potential* short circuit. Similar recall programs have been used to fix a variety of minor or potential problems.

The GM-UAW agreement, emphasizing a commitment to quality, also re-defined the way automobiles are introduced to the market. Saturn uses a unique "market area" approach to emphasize cooperation among retail facilities. First, one dealer owns all facilities, perhaps two or three, within a particular market. Since the facilities have a common owner and are not competing with each other to sell the same car, each facility helps each other serve the customer and build the market. Second, Saturn greatly limits the number of dealers in any one region to avoid market saturation. Where Ford and Chrysler may have thirty or forty dealers competing with each other for the same customer, Saturn may have only two or three. Finally, Saturn dealerships are awarded based on the potential owner's track record in achieving exemplary quality and customer satisfaction standards.

Saturn dealerships often have months-long waiting lists for new cars. This fact, coupled with Saturn's unique customer celebrations and new car clinics, has enabled Saturn to create an almost "clannish" mystique, previously reserved for Harley-Davidson enthusiasts only.

The no-haggle approach to pricing has differentiated Saturn from other nameplates. This is important since the customer does not need to use complex negotiation skills to buy a car, and, more importantly, the customer doesn't leave the dealership wondering if someone else could have gotten a better deal. It's equal opportunity buying at its best—everyone, regardless of age; color; national origin; race; religion; or sex, pays the same price—

no exceptions. In short, the no-haggle approach to pricing reduces the potential for discrimination at the dealership level.

Assembling The Right Team: Competitive Recruiting and Hiring Practices

Saturn dealerships compete aggressively for talent and view their ability to attract excellent employees a competitive advantage. All recruiting and selection efforts are linked to Saturn's service strategy. Turnover rates and the causes of turnover are evaluated periodically. (A workable model for evaluating turnover rates and the causes of turnover is the subject of the next chapter and its associated Technical Appendix.) Once selected, sales consultants are compensated with salaries and bonuses, not commissions. Salaries allow the sales consultant to focus fully on satisfying each customer. Bonuses are based solely on customer satisfaction results. This motivates the sales consultant to strive for *complete,* rather than partial, customer satisfaction.

World-Class Customer Satisfaction And Retention Training Programs

New employee orientation and other training sessions focus on customer satisfaction and retention. All employees are taught and expected to take full responsibility for quality and customer satisfaction. Special, sometimes off-beat, speakers and other methods are incorporated into the training programs to spice things up and to make learning fun. Saturn's training strategy helps bring meaning and energy to the work, stretches each employee to do more, and captures what truly is most valuable to the customer. Saturn's training programs are so highly regarded outside the company, it is now possible for non-Saturn employees to participate in many of the training programs for a reasonable fee.

Results-Oriented Service Evaluations: Don't Just Satisfy Them, Make Them Enthusiastic

Saturn looks for results in customer satisfaction surveys, emphasizing complete, rather than partial, customer satisfaction. In fact, Saturn prefers the term "customer enthusiasm" over "customer satisfaction" and has assembled a Saturn Customer Enthusiasm Team in Troy, Michigan to collect and analyze the survey results. The Springhill, Tennessee headquarters uses the survey results to allocate cars and to determine where additional training is needed; the dealerships use the survey results to track progress and to determine better ways to serve the customer. Rather than treating all results the same, Saturn communicates which results are most important. The goal is to keep all employees focused on "customer enthusiasm" by asking critical questions such as *what product and service characteristics matter most to our customers?* Or, *how well are we doing relative to customer expectations and competitor offerings?*

"If a man does not keep pace with his companions, perhaps it is because he hears a different drummer. Let him step to the music which he hears, however measured or far away."
—Henry David Thoreau

Homer's *Iliad* and the Tuckman Model of Group Development

Key learning from Homer's *Iliad: Similar to Sophocles'* Antigone *in plot, Homer's* Iliad *is dominated by a conflict between Achilles, king of the Myrmidons and greatest warrior in the Achaean (Greek) army, and Agamemnon, king of the Mycenaens and commander-in-chief of the Achaean army, during the final year of the Trojan War. The confrontation between Achilles and Agamemnon over Achilles' war prize, the beautiful captive princess Briseis, and the tragic consequences of that confrontation, forms much of the drama's plot. When Agamemnon publicly takes Briseis as his own, Achilles withdraws the Myrmidons from the war, leaving the Mycenaens to suffer staggering defeats at the hands of the Trojans. Although Achilles eventually returns his forces to the war, Agamemnon's abrasive team-building style nearly results in the destruction of the Achaean army (organization).*

According to the Tuckman Model of Group Development, there are four distinct stages through which a team develops: forming, storming, norming, and performing. Teams encounter unique challenges and problems at each stage of development and require unique organizational strategies to meet the challenges and to solve the problems.

The *forming* stage is a period of orientation and role clarification. During this stage, group members attempt to find which behaviors are acceptable and which are not. The members will remain dependent on management until they find out what the ground rules are and what is expected of them. Essentially, they are testing the limits of the group's authority and responsibility. Employee involvement is limited to the more assertive members of the group. There are many strategies an organization can use to nurture "forming" teams. First, each team should write its own mission statement. This activity goes a long way toward clarifying the team's purpose and focusing the team on a larger unifying goal. Each employee requires a clear understanding of what the organization is trying to achieve. Second, the team should be trained in basic group communication, decision making, listening, and problem solving skills.

The *storming* stage is a period of internal group conflict and disagreement. During this stage, group members assert their individualism and become more assertive in clarifying their roles and what is expected of them. Power struggles surface as more members jockey for center stage, and subgroups based on common interests form. The subgroups may disagree with one another over the group's goals or how to achieve them. Thus, the group is characterized by a general lack of unity. The group's most assertive members still control employee involvement. One strategy an organization can use to nurture "storming" teams is to train all members in group conflict resolution. This activity goes a long way toward encouraging communication and interaction among team members. In addition, it helps clarify each team member's role.

The *norming* stage is a period of role and value clarification. During this stage, conflict is resolved and group unity emerges. Group consensus develops on who has the power, who is the leader, and member's roles. Employee involvement increases as more members come to accept and understand their roles; however, the orientation still is internal. One strategy an organization can use to nurture "norming" teams is to encourage more contact with other groups, including customers and suppliers. This activity goes a long way toward helping teams understand the impact of their efforts on customer value. In addition, it helps focus the group on process improvement efforts.

The *performing* stage is a period of strong unity and performance. During this stage, the major emphasis is on problem solving and accomplishing the assigned task. Members are committed to the group's mission. They are coordinated and confront and resolve problems in the interest of task accomplishment. All employees are involved, contributing to process improvements and taking leadership roles. Everyone has a role in the larger task. One strategy an organization can use to nurture "performing" teams is to provide positive feedback on process improvement efforts and task accomplishments. This activity goes a long way toward focusing team members on the long-term importance of maintaining their strategic relationships and partnerships.

Chapter 11

The Challenge Of The 1990's And Beyond: Attracting, Retaining, And Motivating (ARMing) Quality Employees

"There is nothing permanent except change."

—Heraclitus, Greek philosopher

Natural resources such as clean air and water, metals and minerals, and oil and other fuels are not the only types of resources in short supply. What about human resources—the people who supply the organization with their creativity, drive, and talent? We cannot afford to destroy the creativity, drive, and talent of our precious human resources. Unfortunately, more often than not, we have done just that. Among the most critical tasks of a manager are attracting, retaining, and motivating the people who will best help the organization meet its goals. Without creative, driven, and talented employees, the organization will either pursue inappropriate goals or find it difficult to achieve appropriate goals once they have been set. It's a challenge to attract the appropriate employee. It's an even bigger challenge to keep such an employee motivated. It's an even bigger challenge still to retain such an employee. It is, in fact, the challenge of the 1990s and beyond.

Purpose And Outcomes Of The ARMing Project At Company X*

The purpose of this project is to provide the Leadership Team (top management) with a practical tool for uncovering the source or sources of employee dissatisfaction. Workers influence each other to stay or quit based on their degree of satisfaction or dissatisfaction with various organizational, group, or personal factors. These factors collectively are referred to as the organization's "quality of work life." *Dissatisfaction* with the organization's perceived quality of work life *is a strong motivator for change.* If the organization cannot manage employee dissatisfaction, employees (including the organization's best and brightest) definitely will change— *change organizations, that is.* Thus, the ultimate purpose of this project is to provide the organization with an action plan to "manage" employee dissatisfaction to attract, retain, and motivate the best and brightest employees. The long-term benefits intended to be realized by the successful completion of this project include

- Enhanced effectiveness of the organization as measured by goal attainment.
- Greater customer satisfaction through increased experience and service levels of the organization.
- Improved financial performance.
- Increased job satisfaction.
- More positive attitudes toward the work of the organization and the organization itself.

*The ARMing Project is the actual name of a change project initiated for one of my clients. Throughout this chapter, the organization involved will be referred to as Company X. This has been done at the client's request to protect the actual names of the individuals and the corporations involved. It is important to note that similar projects can be initiated for any organization to determine why it is having difficulty in attracting, retaining, and motivating quality employees.

Background Of The ARMing Project

The Leadership Team is concerned with the long-term impact of high voluntary turnover rates on financial performance, customer satisfaction, and organizational effectiveness. The department currently is experiencing an eleven-percent annual voluntary turnover rate, up from four percent just a year ago. Voluntary turnover is a form of withdrawal from the workplace and occurs when employees permanently quit working for the organization. Voluntary turnover is critical since the organization must spend considerable time and money recruiting, hiring, and training new employees to replace those who leave. Additionally, because workers normally "learn by doing," new workers initially are not as proficient as the people they replace. As a result, strategic projects often are put on hold, key work and group processes are disrupted, and workloads and stress levels increase for those who stay. Most importantly, the customer negatively is affected by the decline in the overall experience and service levels of the organization. Thus, voluntary turnover makes it difficult for the organization to satisfy the intermediate goals and objectives necessary to achieve its mission. These factors have led up to the selection of this particular change project.

Stakeholder Analysis

A stakeholder is any constituency that *perceives* that it will be impacted by a change. The key figures who will be impacted by the proposed changes include the twenty-four member Leadership Team; 138 Service

Center employees; and nearly 584,000 customers representing 5,213 organizations. The Leadership Team stands to gain improved financial performance, greater customer satisfaction, and enhanced organizational effectiveness if the proposed change is implemented as planned. The Leadership Team stands to lose some power through altered task and reporting relationships if the proposed change is implemented as planned. The Service Center's employees stand to gain reduced workloads and stress levels, increased job satisfaction, and greater empowerment through altered task and reporting relationships. Unfortunately, for many of the Service Center's employees, the status quo is comfortable. If the proposed change is implemented as planned, they stand to lose the status quo. *They will be forced to leave their comfort zones.* The customer stands to gain from the increased experience and service levels of the organization in the long term; however, the customer stands to lose a few of the previously-planned service enhancements in the short term. Some of these projects temporarily may have to be placed on hold to free up the financial, human, information, and physical resources necessary to implement the proposed change.

Readiness For Change Estimate Of Company X

The Leadership Team, as a whole, typically exhibits a "reactionary" leadership style. They respond to crisis situations (such as a seemingly-insurmountable voluntary turnover problem) extremely well. The Service Center's employees are aware of the importance of the intended change project for the organization—top management support has been unwavering. Thus, the Leadership Team's level of change readiness for the intended project is high. The level of change readiness among Service Center employees rapidly is increasing from low to high. The potential disadvantage of working with a "reactionary" Leadership Team has been the tendency to foster a dependency on their assistance and expertise. This also may explain why the organization has relied on detailed policies, procedures, and rules rather than on creative and innovative initiatives to respond to rapidly-changing customer needs. The organization's recent movement toward self-directed work teams has increased the expectations and the level of change readiness for the Service Center's employees. The employees see the intended change project as a way to enhance their ability to express their opinions, to listen to the ideas of others, and to respond *pro-actively* to organizational difficulties. Thus, the customers' level of change readiness for the intended project is high—the intended change project should help enhance organizational responsiveness to their needs. Together, the Leadership Team and the Service Center's employees represent the organizational target; the level of change readiness for the organizational target is high. Together, they also represent the organizational sponsor.

Change Approach

I used a basic survey-feedback approach in planning and executing the change project. I gathered, analyzed, summarized, and returned quality of work life data to those who participated in its generation for identification, discussion, and solution of problems. I used the survey-feedback approach for two reasons. First, since workers influence each other to stay or quit based on their degree of satisfaction or dissatisfaction with various quality of work life factors, a survey-feedback approach can be utilized to uncover the source or sources of voluntary turnover. To determine which quality of work life factors were having the most significant impact on voluntary turnover, I developed and used a general statistical model to relate voluntary turnover rates to various quality of work-life factors—values, climate, participation, leadership, and group cohesion, for example. The general statistical model used for this change project was based on multiple linear regression. (The general statistical model, variables, mathematical calculations, and explanations are included in this chapter's Technical

Appendix.) Second, I felt I could reduce resistance by encouraging the active participation and involvement of those affected most by the change project—The Leadership Team and the Service Center's employees—in the generation of recommendations and action plans. The Service Center employees made recommendations to the Leadership Team and the Leadership Team responded with an action plan based on the recommendations.

Event Sequence

Planning Of The Change Project

The first step in the planning of the change project was to define the problem, its background, and its consequences, as well as the purpose and the intended outcomes or benefits of the change project. This step also included the development of a project schedule identifying the items to be done and the planned start/finish dates for each item. Additionally, this step included the development of measurable criteria (or milestones) to determine if each item was complete or on schedule. This first step was necessary to secure top management commitment to the change project. In my opinion, *it's foolish to begin a change project of this magnitude without deep commitment and a defined course of action.* The team needs top management to articulate a simple and concrete, yet compelling vision. From this vision, the communication lines must be opened to obtain agreement on common objectives and expected outcomes. Thus, I helped top management create a vision of the desired future state. This vision served as a source of commitment and motivation. Additionally, it served as an ongoing standard of performance. In short, we made it clear what was expected, defined the consequences of failure or success, and emphasized the sponsor's commitment to the change effort.

The second step in the planning of the change project was an in-depth stakeholder analysis to identify who would be affected and how to deal with them. We started the stakeholder analysis with two questions. First, *What do the various key players want?* Second, *What can we offer each key player to overcome his or her resistance?* To solve potential stakeholder conflicts, we looked for common themes, shared goals, and mutual benefits. In my opinion, *change—whether it's personal or organizational—can be perceived as a problem or as an opportunity. If the stakeholder perceives the change as a problem, you help them solve it. If, on the other hand, the stakeholder perceives the change as an opportunity, you help them take advantage of it.* Each stakeholder is more likely to embrace change if you help them see the project from their unique perspective; however, as I found out, this is not easy. Surprisingly, each stakeholder focused on the potential losses before they focused on the potential gains. These potential losses stimulated resistance, a form of power. Each stakeholder had a basic need or desire to be in control of his or her environment.

Implementation Of The Change Project

The first step in the implementation of the change project was to convert the quality of work life and voluntary turnover rate data into information useful for decision making. This step included the development and application of a multiple linear regression model. I completed the statistical analysis myself, but quickly assembled a small cross-functional team to assist me in the interpretation of the results. In my opinion, *it is much easier to "market" and "sell" the results of such an analysis if others participate in the process.*

The second step in the implementation of the change project was to increase the amount of control in the hands of those affected most by the change—the Leadership Team and the Service Center's employees. In other words, we developed strategies to help each stakeholder maintain control over their environment. In my opinion, *this end often is best achieved by encouraging their active involvement and participation in generating recommendations and action plans.* Involvement and participation help gain alignment and commitment from each stakeholder. Stakeholders are more likely to be aligned with and committed to a change they had some opportunity to help implement. When a change is implemented without stakeholder input, there is much less motivation for the change to be realized. Thus, the change must reflect the interests, abilities, and motivations of all stakeholders. This step culminated in the implementation of an action plan. (See Results Of The ARMing Project)

Assessment Of The Change Project

The first step in the assessment of the change project was to determine how we were going to measure our progress. One measure was whether the change project's actual outcomes matched intended outcomes. The key questions included *did we identify the source or sources of voluntary turnover?* and *were we able to implement an action plan to manage voluntary turnover?* In my opinion, *the ultimate measure of progress is the degree to which the change project affects the ongoing behavior of the organization. In other words, do organizational members decide to stay or leave? Does the change project reduce voluntary turnover?* Unfortunately, the effect of the change project on the "ongoing behavior of the organization" is difficult to measure in just twelve weeks (the amount of time given me to complete the project). The organization will have to track changes in voluntary turnover rates over time.

The second step in the assessment of the change project was the actual measurement of our progress. This step included the elimination or minimization of obstacles, when necessary, to close gaps between actual and intended outcomes. In my opinion, *the organization must monitor the impact of any proposed change on the people (their motivations, perceptions, and skills); the formal organization (the physical environments, the policies and procedures, the strategies, and the structures and technologies); and the informal organization (the norms and values emerging from the ongoing interaction between the people, the formal organization, and the informal organization).* We predicted the effects of the change project on these elements in the stakeholder analysis. This step was necessary to monitor the actual effects.

Results Of The Arming Project

My first achievement was the identification of the three quality of work life factors having the most significant impact on voluntary turnover rates:

◆ Utilize individual strengths, abilities, and talents.
◆ Create opportunities for advancement and growth.
◆ Improve cleanliness, comfort, and safety of physical work environment.

These three factors together explain approximately 95.6% of the total variation in voluntary turnover rates. These three factors quickly became known as the **Associate Retention and Motivation Strategies (ARMS)**.

My second achievement was the establishment of a temporary advisory team of Service Center employees in October to expand on the Associate Retention and Motivation Strategies (ARMS). The advisory team consisted of five members—one employee from each regional service center. Each member was selected by his or her own peers through a consensus decision-making process. Each member was responsible for getting input from and giving feedback to his or her teammates before each advisory team meeting. The purpose of this arrangement was to involve as many people as possible in the recommendation process. This arrangement provided the opportunity for everyone to contribute to and take ownership of the advisory team's recommendations. In November, the Leadership Team responded to the advisory team's recommendations with an action plan (not included as part of this text due to the proprietary nature of the contents of the action plan and my obligation as a consultant to support the stipulations of the confidentiality agreement with Company X.) Thus, the change project's actual outcomes matched the intended outcomes—the identification of the source or sources of voluntary turnover and the implementation of an action plan to manage voluntary turnover. A copy of the employee memo that accompanied the recommendations to the Leadership Team is included below.

Promotion opportunities influence our development and growth; however, with fewer promotional opportunities available due to leaner management staffs, strategies for coping with the voluntary turnover problem must focus more on the importance of challenge than on the importance of promotion. In other words, one way to encourage personal growth and development in the absence of promotional opportunities is to make our existing jobs more challenging and more satisfying.

In addition, we expect to be rewarded for superior performance. In the past, superior performance often was rewarded with the opportunity of promotion. Today, the organization can reward superior performance with more challenging jobs. One way to accomplish this is to adjust work responsibilities to fit our individual strengths, abilities, and talents. Another way is to encourage lateral transfers to other jobs or departments within the organization to promote the development of new skills.

We are hungry for opportunities to develop and to grow in our jobs. We crave opportunities for advancement. We crave opportunities to develop and to use new competencies to accomplish the work of the organization. If we cannot find opportunities for development and growth in this organization, we will seek them in another.

> Lastly, the organization must promote a healthy physical work environment by maintaining comfortable atmospheric conditions and providing workplace safety and security. We should be allowed to "personalize" our work areas to create "nests" for creativity and innovation. By influencing the physical work environment, the organization can enhance productivity and the retention of valued employees.
>
> Enthusiastically,
> Company X Employees

One non-intended consequence was the Leadership Team's adamant opposition to the advisory team's *physical work environment* recommendations. (This opposition primarily was driven by budgetary concerns and constraints.) Many of the Service Center's employees stated they do not enjoy coming to work since they do not feel comfortable in the "stale and stuffy" physical work environment and would like the opportunity to "personalize their work areas to create nests for creativity and innovation." To date, the on-going battle over the physical work environment has overshadowed the significance of the career development action plan.

To some extent, this dilemma can be explained by Maslow's Hierarchy of Needs. According to psychologist Abraham Maslow, human beings have a variety of needs, some more fundamental or basic than others. Maslow grouped these needs into five categories, arranged in a hierarchy from lower deficiency needs (physiological, security, belongingness) and higher growth needs (esteem, self-actualization). Deficiency needs dominate behavior until they are satisfied. Once satisfied, an individual begins the move up the hierarchy to focus on growth needs. Thus, it is possible the career development action plan (a growth need) will not take center stage until the physical work environment (a deficiency need) is satisfied.

Key Learning From The ARMing Project

The long-term competitive position of any organization is determined by its ability to create value from multiple perspectives—customer, employee, and management. Every organization, in fact, is a value-delivery system. Thus, any change project must provide superior stakeholder value and provide the organization with better ways to meet or exceed their stakeholders' needs and expectations.

"The best way to predict the future is to invent it."
—Alan Kay, Fellow at Apple Computer and inventor of the Macintosh interface

Conclusions

"We must stop talking about the American Dream and start listening to the dreams of Americans"

—Reubin Askew, former governor of Florida

Leadership, Capital, Labor, And Economic Performance

Americans are losing faith in their ability to prosper. In the introduction of this book, I stated "…the missing element for long-term competitiveness is leadership." In fact, the number one reason for all new business failures in America is the lack of bold, decisive, and visionary leadership in business and government. Leaders make the decisions (or empower others to make the decisions) that create problems or opportunities for our society. Unfortunately, our existing leadership has created more problems than opportunities, and, thus, serves as the single largest obstacle to the American Dream.

In addition to the leadership obstacle, the American Dream has a capital obstacle and a labor obstacle. Poor leadership, combined with a lack of capital for long-term investment and an inadequate primary and secondary public school system, translates into sub-par economic performance.

Yes, it's true economic growth is the engine of opportunity and prosperity; however, capital is the fuel of economic growth. *Without fuel, the engine cannot run.* Corporations need capital to build inventory to levels required to generate the sales projected under the business forecast, to renovate or modernize the physical plant, to add or replace needed fixtures and equipment, to finance accounts receivable, to provide planned advertising or promotional launch programs, and to maintain adequate working capital. Next to poor leadership, lack of adequate working capital—a phenomenon known as under-capitalization—is the single largest obstacle to the American Dream. Ancient empires—Sumerian, Egyptian, Babylonian, Chinese, Greek, Roman, and Venetian—collapsed because they failed to reinvest the fruits of prosperity to generate more capital for expansion and growth. All past civilizations have died because of self-imposed boundaries beyond which they did not permit themselves to go. The United States has developed an economic empire unparalleled in human history. Unfortunately, our under-capitalized empire is collapsing under the weight of a ballooning trade deficit; a crushing tax burden; decaying, crime-ridden cities; an escalating number of personal-bankruptcy filings; failing school systems; an economically- and morally-bankrupt welfare state; mounting consumer debt as a percentage of disposable income; onerous government regulations; soaring energy costs; a spiraling national debt; and wasteful government spending. *Capitalism without capital is merely an ism. To survive and prosper, America must put the capital back into capitalism.*

Reducing the cost of labor is not the answer. If it is, it must have been a really stupid question. The fact is, well-paid employees can afford to purchase the products they produce; poorly-paid one's can't. (Nor can robots, for that matter.) Firms with well-paid employees, all other things being equal, have substantially-higher productivity rates since the employees are energized and excited about producing something they too can own. *Purpose, coupled with the opportunity for ownership, is a powerful motivator.* Organizations that can attract, retain, and motivate (ARM) quality employees have a competitive advantage over those that cannot. Unfortunately, too many American workers lack the skills necessary to perform today's knowledge-intensive jobs, thanks to a public education system that fundamentally is out of step with the larger economic and social realities of a global economy. Compounding this problem, too many American employers lack the appropriate working environment, tools, and leadership necessary to ARM quality employees anyway. Once again, America's failure to invest in human capital has damaged our ability to compete.

We stand at a historic crossroads; we have a choice. We can continue down the same path of self-destruction and self-annihilation. Or, we can shift direction and create an opportunity society with more-abundant capital and better-skilled labor.

Downsizing And Outsourcing

Downsizing is a disease that devastates employee morale and hampers the organization's ability to grow. Downsizing may cut costs in the short-term, but at the expense of the people who have the potential to create value for the organization in the long term. What is needed is leadership capable of releasing this potential, capable of eliminating or minimizing obstacles to value delivery. Cutting people alone is inadequate. Improved financial performance, greater customer satisfaction, and enhanced organizational effectiveness only can be achieved with continuous, fundamental changes in leadership and core business processes. High-performing organizations succeed by re-designing organizational structures and systems to satisfy an employee's basic needs for the right working environment, the right tools, and the right leadership.

Not only do employees have basic needs for the right working environment, the right tools, and the right leadership, they have basic needs to be in control of their environment and to reduce uncertainty. This holds true whether multiple needs motivate behavior simultaneously (Murray) or in some preset order, or hierarchy (Maslow).

On the flip side, downsizing has created new opportunities for individuals. While many Americans are shutting themselves up inside their homes to protect themselves from the harsh, unpredictable realities of the outside world, still many more are forming businesses of their own to take control of their own destinies. *Ultimately, downsizing will intensify the competitive battlefield of the future...employees today, competitors tomorrow.*

In search of a quick fix to the financial performance problem, numerous organizations have indiscriminately outsourced employees and functions to reduce costs. They've failed to distinguish between high-value added, low-value added, and non-value added employees and functions. What's worse, they've misidentified their true purpose or their true customer. High-performing organizations, on the other hand, have outsourced employees and functions only after putting themselves through the following three-step process:

A. Establish a clear and commonly-understood purpose and identify the major lines of business and strategic activities the organization will develop to fulfill its purpose, as well as the critical success factors of the industry.

B. Identify the core processes necessary to accomplish your purpose and establish the critical success indicators the organization will use to track its progress.

C. Overhaul the organization's culture and structure to support the achievement of the organization's purpose.

Middle-income Americans are falling far short of fulfilling their dreams. Why? They've allowed others to control their destinies. They've left their jobs and career security to chance. They've failed to take control of their lives and to live their dreams. Since they didn't, someone else did. It's time for Middle-income Americans to manage their own job and career security, to seek out the opportunities that surround change, to develop new skills, and to prepare themselves for industry upswings and downswings. By doing this, they enhance their employability and make their futures more secure.

The government has served as our most visible obstacle to the American Dream. By taxing or subsidizing things it shouldn't, the government creates the environment for us to borrow more than we save, consume more than we produce, spend more money than we earn, and redistribute wealth rather than create it. Jack Kemp, former United States Representative and founder and co-director of Empower America, a public policy and advocacy organization, stated it best:

> "If you tax something, you get less of it. If you subsidize something, you get more of it. The problem in America today is that we are taxing work, saving, investment, and productivity; and we're subsidizing debt, welfare, consumption, leisure, and mediocrity."

In addition to taxing and subsidizing the wrong things, the government measures its progress using deceptive statistics, including the unemployment rate. Franklin County, Ohio, for example, has a low unemployment rate; however, it has a high *under*employment rate…food service workers with college degrees, for example. The point is, the low unemployment rate does not paint an accurate picture of the State of the Union. It does not have to end this way. The government has the potential to unleash the job creation machine and to reinvent itself:

√Adopt conservative fiscal management policies.
√Change outmoded accounting standards.
√Cut foreign aid and invest in America first.
√Develop a new "Made in USA" labeling system.
√Elect competent leaders who add value to our society.
√Encourage American labor unions to organize labor in foreign nations, especially in Mexico.

√End world dependence on Middle-Eastern oil.

√Fortify the nation's infrastructure.

√Foster partnerships between American businesses and university laboratories, between science and industry.

√Make all pensions and health-care programs portable.

√Make the government adhere to the same accounting principles and standards it imposes on American corporations.

√Overhaul the guidelines for immigration to America.

√Place a cap on the amount of restructuring charges a corporation can take against income in a single year.

√Put an end to America's unilateral free-trade policies.

√Put and end to life-time appointments to the Supreme Court.

√Reduce barriers to new enterprise and stimulate entrepreneurial initiative by altering the tax code.

√Reduce the regulatory bureaucracy and put an end to frivolous lawsuits.

√Reinvent government by privatizing operations and downsizing.

√Require foreign corporations doing business in America to pay the same tax rates and to comply with the same regulations as American corporations.

√Shift welfare funding into jobs programs, requiring work for benefits.

√Upgrade public education and establish a national apprentice program to replace vocational training.

A Final Call To Action

Whatever happened to the insatiable American spirit—the spirit of the Eagle—that unabashedly arose to the occasion to accept challenges and to take initiatives to overcome obstacles? The Japanese, for example, do not hide their trade barriers, but rather they overtly hang them out in front of us, taunting us, challenging us, to find ways to overcome them. What's stopping us from finding ways to overcome them? I say if we can get a man to the moon and back, we can accomplish anything we set our hearts, minds, and spirits too. We must begin once again to solve our problems and to take advantage of our opportunities. We must look back to see old patterns and look ahead to seize new potentials. It's time for us to unlock our full potential by rethinking the way we think. Our future does not exist. We create it. Together, we can keep the American Dream alive.

"The true American Dream not only provides the freedom to use our gifts and talents to achieve our highest goals, but also the freedom to fulfill our purpose in life."
—David McNally, author of *Even Eagles Need A Push*

*   *   *

Eagles, spread thy wings.

*   *   *

About the Author

Christopher England, a finance and marketing professional, is an accomplished management and process improvement consultant. His clients have included Columbia Gas of Ohio, the Columbus Museum of Art, Franklin University, and Nationwide Insurance in Columbus, Ohio; Kent State University in Kent, Ohio; Laurel Lake Conference Center in Pataskala, Ohio; and Online Computer Library Center (OCLC) in Dublin, Ohio, to name just but a few. Some of his more creative projects have included a local marketing plan for the Columbus Museum of Art's nationally-recognized *1st Thursdays* and an international marketing plan for OCLC's 21st release of the *Dewey Decimal Classification System*, the world's largest library and knowledge classification system. His audiences range from senior executives to middle managers, from seasoned professionals to entry-level support staff.

Mr. England obtained his MBA in Organizational Leadership and Management from Franklin University in Columbus, Ohio in December 1995. Chris, a summa cum laude graduate of Kent State University in Kent, Ohio, also holds a BBA in Human Resources Management and Business Management. As a student at Kent State University, he received Distinguished Cadet honors as a Technical Sergeant in the Air Force Reserve Officer Training Corps, and was a recipient of the Reserve Officers Association of the United States Award in acknowledgment of his "meritorious contribution to the common good of the United States." He holds his National Association of Securities Dealers (NASD) Series 6 license and is an active member of the Society of Competitive Intelligence Professionals (SCIP). Chris has hands-on experience in applying business and market intelligence and counterintelligence to corporate strategy, and has undergone intensive training at John Nolan and William DeGenaro's Centre for Operational Business Intelligence in Sarasota, FL. He resides in Pickerington, Ohio.

Appendix

Technical Appendix to Chapter 11

General Statistical Model

This research was undertaken to examine the impact of various independent variables on voluntary turnover rates. I developed and fit a multiple linear regression model relating voluntary turnover rates (Y, stated in percentage terms) to twenty-four independent variables for a sample n = 17 departments at Company X. The twenty-four independent variables used in this analysis as predictors of Y were

◆ (X1) I'm encouraged to improve my performance through additional training and education

◆ (X2) Management is firm, fair, and honest in dealing with associates

◆ (X3) Input from associates is asked for and used when management is considering changes in company policies and procedures

◆ (X4) There is a real sense of teamwork and cooperation within my department

◆ (X5) My strengths, abilities, and talents are being utilized in my current job

◆ (X6) The benefits package is flexible enough to meet my needs

- (X7) Good performance is rewarded in this organization
- (X8) I am respected by my coworkers for my ability to do my job
- (X9) My company provides the necessary resources to get the job done
- (X10) I am satisfied with the recognition and respect I am receiving for the work I am now doing
- (X11) My supervisor trusts us
- (X12) I am satisfied with my opportunities for advancement and growth
- (X13) I am satisfied with my physical work environment; it is clean, comfortable, and safe
- (X14) I have the opportunity to make important contributions to the success of this company
- (X15) My boss encourages and welcomes new ideas on how to improve our company
- (X16) My job is interesting and challenging
- (X17) The pay for my position is fair based on what other organizations in the area are paying for similar positions
- (X18) I receive regular feedback about my performance in relation to goals
- (X19) I am given the freedom and flexibility to make decisions relevant to my job activities
- (X20) I am compensated fairly for the work I do
- (X21) I have had adequate on-the-job training to perform according to company standards
- (X22) My company offers stability, security, and risk as needed
- (X23) Company policies and procedures are communicated clearly and applied consistently throughout the company
- (X24) The amount of overtime I have to work to get my job done is reasonable

For my study, I utilized the average scores from the 1995 Company X Quality of Work Life (QWL) Survey for each department. The departmental survey results and voluntary turnover rates were obtained through the Department of Human Resources. Each survey question measured the degree of agreement/satisfaction or disagreement/dissatisfaction:

- 1 Strongly Disagree
- 2 Usually Disagree
- 3 Somewhat Disagree
- 4 Somewhat Agree
- 5 Usually Agree
- 6 Strongly Agree

The objective of this study was to find the best-fitting multiple linear regression model of the form

$$\hat{y} = b_0 + b_1 x_1 + b_2 x_2 + b_3 x_3 \bullet \bullet \bullet b_{24} x_{24}$$

to describe the relationship, if any, between voluntary turnover rates (Y) and the independent variables X1, X2, X3, • • • X24. I modeled various combinations of the independent variables; each model provided a least squares estimate and an F-ratio. By studying the least squares estimate in combination with the F-ratio it is possible to draw conclusions about the population in question with a known risk of error. The F-ratio provides a test of the hypothesis

$$H_0: B1 = B2 = B3 \bullet \bullet \bullet B24 = 0$$

that is, a test of whether or not there is a relation between Y and the independent variables X1, X2, X3 • • • X24. Associated with each F-ratio is a p-value. The p-value is the exact or known risk of error; it is the probability of being wrong if you say the least squares equation applies to the population. In other words, p-values allow us to assess the significance of F-test results without resorting to complicated tables. If you fail to reject the null hypothesis there is no relation between Y and the independent variables. If, however, B1; B2; B3 • • • B24 are not all equal to zero (thus allowing the rejection of H_0) a relation does exist between Y and at least one of the independent variables.

Progress To Better Least Squares Estimates

Steps prior to multiple linear regression analysis:

Step 1:   Developed a pool of potentially-useful independent variables.
Step 2:   Established the criteria for evaluation of the models.
The criteria I established were that of minimizing the p-value and maximizing the coefficient of determination (r^2) for the regression model.
Step 3:   Modeled each independent variable separately by holding the rest of the equation constant.
Step 4:   Eliminated from further study all variables that did not meet a minimum r^2 of .450 or a maximum p-value of .005.

Variables that did not meet my limits included X3, X6, X7, X8, X10, X11, X17, X19, X20, X21, X23, and X24. All other variables met my requirements.

After the criteria of minimizing the p-value and maximizing the r^2 led to several "good" regression models, I chose the "best" regression model.

Model 1: Modeled independent variables X5 and X12. This model explained 85.9% (r^2) of the variation in Y. X5's p-value increased by .088

and X12's p-value increased by .007. I chose to start with X5 and X12 because of the outstanding results they displayed when modeled individually—both had p-values of .000.

Model 2: Added X22 to Model 1 to see if it had any positive effects on the p-value's of X5 and X12. This model explained an additional 5.3% of the variation in Y explained by Model 1. X5's p-value improved by .083. X12's improved by .006, while X22's increased by .015. I added X22 because of its outstanding p-value of .000.

Model 3: Added X13 to Model 2 to see if I could improve the results enough to warrant keeping any of the variables. The results of this model were rather disappointing; by adding X13, I only was able to improve r^2 by 5.2%. X13's p-value increased by .001. The addition of X13 also forced the p-values of X5 and X22 to worsen. The p-value of X12 remained unchanged.

Model 4: Dropped X13 from Model 2 and added X18. This model explained 3.9% less of the variation in Y explained by Model 3. X22's p-value improved by .077, while X5's, X12's, and X18's increased by a small amount each. I dropped X13 due to its poor influence on X22. I added X18 to bring its low p-value of .000 into the model.

Model 5: Dropped X18 from Model 4 and added X15. This model explained an additional .6% of the variation in Y explained by Model 4. However, X5's and X12's p-values increased by .037 and .021, respectively. X15's p-value increased by .093, while X22's improved by .008. Even though X18 improved the model dramatically, I was not overly-impressed by the results. I decided on X15 due to its outstanding p-value of .000.

Model 6: Dropped X15 and X22 from Model 5 and placed X18 back into the equation. Although this model explained 3.9% less of the variation in Y explained by Model 5, I was more pleased with the p-values of the individual variables. X12's p-value improved by .006 and X18's p-value improved by .106 (see Model 4). However, X5's p-value increased by .067.

Model 7: Dropped X18 from Model 6 and placed X15 back into the equation. This helped to explain an additional .6% of the variation in Y explained by Model 6. X5's p-value increased from .118 to .414 and X12's p-value increased somewhat over the previous model.

Model 8: Dropped X15 from Model 7 and placed X13 back into the equation. This model explained more of the variation in Y than any other model since Model 3—95.6%. The p-values for all three variables—X5, X12, and X13—improved dramatically.

My strategy in moving from model to model was to not only maximize r^2, but to minimize the model's overall p-value while still maintaining good p-values for each independent variable in the model. If improving r^2 and the model's overall p-value impaired the p-values of the independent variables in the model, I used one of three methods for developing a better model:

1) I added new variables to the equation
2) I dropped variables from the equation
3) I added previously-dropped variables back into the equation

Method three was possible due to the limited number of variables that met my restrictive requirements. I chose to drop and add variables X15 and X18, numerous times throughout the analysis due to the closeness of their individual results—both had p-values of .000 and an r^2 within .054 of each other. It was difficult to find other variables that had individual results this close together. All three methods enabled me to move progressively and smoothly toward my "best" model.

I chose the model with variables X5, X12, and X13 as my "best" model. According to this model, voluntary turnover rates are influenced most by the extent to which an individual's strengths, abilities, and talents are being utilized on the job; the opportunities for growth and advancement; and the quality of the physical work environment. The least squares equation for this model is

$$\hat{Y} = 13.626 + 2.457X5 - 3.263X12 - 1.425X13$$

This equation predicts that the departmental voluntary turnover rates should, in fact, range between 0 and 11%. The 0% voluntary turnover rate can be achieved if individual strengths, abilities, and talents are being utilized; there are many opportunities for advancement and growth; and the physical work environment is clean, comfortable, and safe. bX5 predicts that for every increase in employee satisfaction levels with individual strength, ability, and talent utilization, the voluntary turnover rate will increase by 2.457%. Thus, a department that utilizes individual strengths, abilities, and talents can realize as much as a 14.74% increase in the voluntary turnover rate. bX12 predicts that for every increase in employee satisfaction levels with departmental opportunities for advancement and growth, the voluntary turnover rate will decline by 3.263%. Thus, a department that offers many opportunities for advancement and growth can improve their voluntary turnover rate by as much as 19.58%. bX13 predicts that for every increase in employee satisfaction levels with the physical work environment , the voluntary turnover rate will decline by 1.425%. Thus, a department offering a clean, comfortable, and safe physical work environment can improve their voluntary turnover rate by as much as 8.55%.

The F-ratio is 94.195 and the associated p-value is .000. This p-value indicates that the value of F = 94.195 is very highly significant. Thus, we can reject the null hypothesis:

$$H_0: B5 = B12 = B13 = 0$$

This provides strong evidence that this model contributes substantial information for the prediction of Y.

The coefficient of multiple determination (r^2) is a measure of the combined effect of all independent variables in the regression model (X5, X12, and X13) in reducing the variability in Y (voluntary turnover rates). A small r^2 means that X5, X12, and X13 contribute very little information for prediction of Y; a large r^2 means that X5, X12, and X13 contribute much information for prediction of Y. The proportion of variation in voluntary turnover rates explained by this model is r^2 = .956. Thus, approximately 95.6% of the total variation in Y can be explained by the terms in this model. The remainder, 4.4%, is left unexplained.

Before I started analyzing my data, I was biased toward a model that consisted of X6 (benefits), X7 (recognition and rewards), X12 (promotional opportunities), and X14 (the opportunity to make important contributions). I felt, in my mind, that these variables were the "best" predictors of voluntary turnover rates. Once I started my analysis, I discovered my first instincts to be wrong. X6 and X7 displayed poor individual results and did not meet my minimum requirements. Thus, these variables were not included in any of the models. X12 and X14 were closely correlated—individuals who "saw" more opportunities for advancement and growth, also "saw" more opportunities to make important contributions—and I decided to use X12 in the models over X14. The use of X12 allowed me to move smoothly from one model to the next. Through my study, I determined that organizations should focus on utilizing the strengths, abilities, and talents of their employees; creating more opportunities for advancement and growth; and improving the cleanliness, comfort, and safety of the physical work environment.

*   *   *

CASE	X1	X2	X3	X4	X5	X6	X7	X8	X9
1	5.000	5.000	4.000	5.000	6.000	5.000	5.000	4.000	6.000
2	4.000	4.000	3.000	3.000	2.000	5.000	5.000	4.000	4.000
3	5.000	5.000	5.000	5.000	5.000	5.000	6.000	4.000	5.000
4	4.000	4.000	4.000	4.000	3.000	5.000	4.000	4.000	4.000
5	5.000	5.000	5.000	5.000	5.000	5.000	6.000	4.000	5.000
6	4.000	2.000	4.000	4.000	2.000	5.000	2.000	4.000	3.000
7	5.000	4.000	5.000	4.000	4.000	5.000	4.000	4.000	5.000
8	5.000	4.000	4.000	5.000	5.000	5.000	5.000	4.000	5.000
9	5.000	2.000	3.000	4.000	1.000	5.000	3.000	4.000	4.000
10	5.000	5.000	4.000	4.000	4.000	5.000	5.000	4.000	6.000
11	5.000	5.000	4.000	5.000	6.000	5.000	5.000	4.000	5.000
12	5.000	4.000	4.000	4.000	3.000	5.000	5.000	4.000	6.000
13	5.000	4.000	5.000	5.000	3.000	5.000	5.000	4.000	6.000
14	5.000	5.000	4.000	5.000	5.000	5.000	5.000	4.000	5.000
15	5.000	4.000	3.000	4.000	3.000	5.000	4.000	4.000	5.000
16	5.000	5.000	4.000	5.000	5.000	5.000	5.000	4.000	6.000
17	5.000	4.000	4.000	4.000	4.000	5.000	5.000	4.000	5.000

*   *   *

CASE	X10	X11	X12	X13	X14	X15	X16	X17	X18
1	4.000	4.000	6.000	6.000	6.000	5.000	6.000	5.000	5.000
2	4.000	3.000	1.000	3.000	1.000	2.000	2.000	5.000	4.000
3	3.000	4.000	5.000	5.000	5.000	5.000	5.000	4.000	5.000
4	4.000	4.000	3.000	4.000	3.000	4.000	3.000	4.000	4.000
5	3.000	4.000	5.000	5.000	5.000	5.000	5.000	4.000	5.000
6	4.000	4.000	2.000	2.000	2.000	3.000	2.000	4.000	4.000
7	4.000	4.000	4.000	4.000	4.000	5.000	4.000	4.000	5.000
8	4.000	4.000	5.000	5.000	5.000	4.000	5.000	4.000	5.000
9	4.000	4.000	1.000	3.000	1.000	3.000	1.000	4.000	4.000
10	4.000	4.000	4.000	5.000	4.000	6.000	4.000	5.000	5.000
11	3.000	4.000	6.000	5.000	6.000	5.000	6.000	4.000	5.000
12	4.000	4.000	3.000	5.000	3.000	4.000	3.000	5.000	5.000
13	4.000	4.000	3.000	5.000	3.000	6.000	3.000	5.000	5.000
14	3.000	4.000	5.000	5.000	5.000	5.000	5.000	4.000	5.000
15	4.000	4.000	3.000	5.000	3.000	5.000	3.000	4.000	5.000
16	3.000	4.000	5.000	6.000	5.000	5.000	5.000	5.000	5.000
17	4.000	4.000	4.000	5.000	4.000	5.000	4.000	4.000	5.000

*   *   *

CASE	X19	X20	X21	X22	X23	X24	Y
1	5.000	5.000	5.000	5.000	5.000	3.000	1.000
2	3.000	5.000	4.000	2.000	6.000	6.000	11.000
3	5.000	4.000	5.000	5.000	5.000	5.000	3.000
4	4.000	5.000	4.000	3.000	4.000	4.000	4.000
5	5.000	4.000	5.000	5.000	5.000	5.000	3.000
6	5.000	1.000	3.000	1.000	1.000	4.000	10.000
7	5.000	5.000	4.000	4.000	5.000	5.000	3.500
8	4.000	3.000	4.000	5.000	5.000	5.000	2.500
9	4.000	5.000	4.000	1.000	4.000	3.000	9.000
10	4.000	5.000	4.000	4.000	6.000	3.000	3.500
11	4.000	3.000	5.000	6.000	6.000	4.000	1.000
12	5.000	5.000	5.000	3.000	5.000	3.000	4.000
13	5.000	5.000	5.000	3.000	5.000	3.000	4.000
14	5.000	3.000	5.000	5.000	4.000	3.000	2.500
15	5.000	5.000	4.000	3.000	5.000	5.000	4.000
16	5.000	5.000	4.000	6.000	4.000	3.000	1.000
17	5.000	4.000	4.000	4.000	5.000	4.000	3.500

*   *   *

TOTAL OBSERVATIONS: 17

	X1	X2	X3	X4	X5
N OF CASES	17	17	17	17	17
MINIMUM	4.000	2.000	3.000	3.000	1.000
MAXIMUM	5.000	5.000	5.000	5.000	6.000
MEAN	4.824	4.176	4.059	4.412	3.882
STANDARD DEV	0.393	0.951	0.659	0.618	1.453

	X6	X7	X8	X9	X10
N OF CASES	17	17	17	17	17
MINIMUM	5.000	2.000	4.000	3.000	3.000
MAXIMUM	5.000	6.000	4.000	6.000	4.000
MEAN	5.000	4.647	4.000	5.000	3.706
STANDARD DEV	0.000	0.996	0.000	0.866	0.470

	X11	X12	X13	X14	X15
N OF CASES	17	17	17	17	17
MINIMUM	3.000	1.000	2.000	1.000	2.000
MAXIMUM	4.000	6.000	6.000	6.000	6.000
MEAN	3.941	3.824	4.588	3.824	4.529
STANDARD DEV	0.243	1.551	1.064	1.551	1.068

	X16	X17	X18	X19	X20
N OF CASES	17	17	17	17	17
MINIMUM	1.000	4.000	4.000	3.000	1.000
MAXIMUM	6.000	5.000	5.000	5.000	5.000
MEAN	3.882	4.353	4.765	4.588	4.235
STANDARD DEV	1.453	0.493	0.437	0.618	1.147

	X21	X22	X23	X24	Y
N OF CASES	17	17	17	17	17
MINIMUM	3.000	1.000	1.000	3.000	1.000
MAXIMUM	5.000	6.000	6.000	6.000	11.000
MEAN	4.353	3.824	4.706	4.000	4.147
STANDARD DEV	0.606	1.551	1.160	1.000	2.999

*   *   *

DEP VAR: Y N: 17 MULTIPLE R: .927 SQUARED MULTIPLE R: .859

ADJUSTED SQUARED MULTIPLE R: .838 STANDARD ERROR OF ESTIMATE: 1.206

VARIABLE	COEFFICIENT	STD ERROR	STD COEF	TOLERANCE	T	P (2 TAIL)
CONSTANT	9.985	0.931	0.000		10.729	0.000
X5	2.581	1.407	1.250	0.0217370	1.834	0.088
X12	-4.148	1.318	-2.145	0.0217370	-3.146	0.007

ANALYSIS OF VARIANCE

SOURCE	SUM-OF-SQUARES	DF	MEAN-SQUARE	F-RATIO	P
REGRESSION	123.531	2	61.766	42.490	0.000
RESIDUAL	20.351	14	1.454		

* * *

DEP VAR: Y N: 17 MULTIPLE R: .955 SQUARED MULTIPLE R: .912

ADJUSTED SQUARED MULTIPLE R: .891 STANDARD ERROR OF ESTIMATE: 0.988

VARIABLE	COEFFICIENT	STD ERROR	STD COEF	TOLERANCE	T	P (2 TAIL)
CONSTANT	9.668	0.771	0.000		12.534	0.000
X5	4.468	1.336	2.165	0.0162032	3.344	0.005
X12	-4.358	1.083	-2.253	0.0216331	-4.022	0.001
X22	-1.623	0.580	-0.839	0.0754906	-2.799	0.015

ANALYSIS OF VARIANCE

SOURCE	SUM-OF-SQUARES	DF	MEAN-SQUARE	F-RATIO	P
REGRESSION	131.185	3	43.728	44.770	0.000
RESIDUAL	12.697	13	0.977		

* * *

DEP VAR: Y   N: 17   MULTIPLE R: .982   SQUARED MULTIPLE R: .964

ADJUSTED SQUARED MULTIPLE R: .953   STANDARD ERROR OF ESTIMATE: 0.653

VARIABLE	COEFFICIENT	STD ERROR	STD COEF	TOLERANCE	T	P (2 TAIL)
CONSTANT	12.894	0.919	0.000		14.025	0.000
X5	3.333	0.923	1.615	0.0148244	3.612	0.004
X12	-3.501	0.744	-1.810	0.0200205	-4.706	0.001
X13	-1.195	0.283	-0.424	0.2928809	-4.217	0.001
X22	-0.737	0.437	-0.381	0.0580195	-1.686	0.118

ANALYSIS OF VARIANCE

SOURCE	SUM-OF-SQUARES	DF	MEAN-SQUARE	F-RATIO	P
REGRESSION	138.766	4	34.692	81.367	0.000
RESIDUAL	5.116	12	0.426		

*   *   *

DEP VAR: Y   N: 17   MULTIPLE R: .962   SQUARED MULTIPLE R: .925

ADJUSTED SQUARED MULTIPLE R: .900   STANDARD ERROR OF ESTIMATE: 0.949

VARIABLE	COEFFICIENT	STD ERROR	STD COEF	TOLERANCE	T	P (2 TAIL)
CONSTANT	14.969	3.728	0.000		4.016	0.002
X5	3.870	1.347	1.875	0.0146848	2.872	0.014
X12	-3.783	1.113	-1.956	0.0188902	-3.399	0.005
X18	-1.308	0.901	-0.191	0.3623358	-1.451	0.172
X22	-1.348	0.588	-0.697	0.0676104	-2.291	0.041

ANALYSIS OF VARIANCE

SOURCE	SUM-OF-SQUARES	DF	MEAN-SQUARE	F-RATIO	P
REGRESSION	133.080	4	33.270	36.960	0.000
RESIDUAL	10.802	12	0.900		

*   *   *

DEP VAR: Y   N: 17   MULTIPLE R: .965   SQUARED MULTIPLE R: .931

ADJUSTED SQUARED MULTIPLE R: .908   STANDARD ERROR OF ESTIMATE: 0.910

VARIABLE	COEFFICIENT	STD ERROR	STD COEF	TOLERANCE	T	P (2 TAIL)
CONSTANT	11.761	1.349	0.000		8.718	0.000
X5	3.114	1.437	1.508	0.0118798	2.167	0.051
X12	-3.093	1.215	-1.599	0.0145941	-2.547	0.026
X15	-0.608	0.333	-0.216	0.4097954	-1.826	0.093
X22	-1.340	0.556	-0.693	0.0696088	-2.410	0.033

ANALYSIS OF VARIANCE

SOURCE	SUM-OF-SQUARES	DF	MEAN-SQUARE	F-RATIO	P
REGRESSION	133.945	4	33.486	40.435	0.000
RESIDUAL	9.938	12	0.828		

*   *   *

DEP VAR: Y   N: 17   MULTIPLE R: .945   SQUARED MULTIPLE R: .892

ADJUSTED SQUARED MULTIPLE R: .867   STANDARD ERROR OF ESTIMATE: 1.093

VARIABLE	COEFFICIENT	STD ERROR	STD COEF	TOLERANCE	T	P (2 TAIL)
CONSTANT	17.909	4.031	0.000		4.443	0.001
X5	2.162	1.293	1.047	0.0211701	1.672	0.118
X12	-3.333	1.262	-1.724	0.0194954	-2.642	0.020
X18	-1.975	0.982	-0.288	0.4045673	-2.010	0.066

ANALYSIS OF VARIANCE

SOURCE	SUM-OF-SQUARES	DF	MEAN-SQUARE	F-RATIO	P
REGRESSION	128.357	3	42.786	35.826	0.000
RESIDUAL	15.525	13	1.194		

*   *   *

DEP VAR: Y   N: 17   MULTIPLE R: .947   SQUARED MULTIPLE R: .898

ADJUSTED SQUARED MULTIPLE R: .874   STANDARD ERROR OF ESTIMATE: 1.065

VARIABLE	COEFFICIENT	STD ERROR	STD COEF	TOLERANCE	T	P (2 TAIL)
CONSTANT	12.775	1.500	0.000		8.515	0.000
X5	1.178	1.394	0.571	0.0172805	0.845	0.414
X12	-2.467	1.389	-1.276	0.0152928	-1.777	0.099
X15	-0.832	0.374	-0.296	0.4444220	-2.223	0.045

ANALYSIS OF VARIANCE

SOURCE	SUM-OF-SQUARES	DF	MEAN-SQUARE	F-RATIO	P
REGRESSION	129.136	3	43.045	37.948	0.000
RESIDUAL	14.746	13	1.134		

*   *   *

DEP VAR: Y   N: 17   MULTIPLE R: .978   SQUARED MULTIPLE R: .956

ADJUSTED SQUARED MULTIPLE R: .946   STANDARD ERROR OF ESTIMATE: 0.698

VARIABLE	COEFFICIENT	STD ERROR	STD COEF	TOLERANCE	T	P (2 TAIL)
CONSTANT	13.626	0.866	0.000		15.734	0.000
X5	2.457	0.815	1.190	0.0217194	3.015	0.010
X12	-3.263	0.781	-1.687	0.0207675	-4.181	0.001
X13	-1.425	0.266	-0.506	0.3810741	-5.367	0.000

ANALYSIS OF VARIANCE

SOURCE	SUM-OF-SQUARES	DF	MEAN-SQUARE	F-RATIO	P
REGRESSION	137.554	3	45.851	94.195	0.000
RESIDUAL	6.328	13	0.487		

*   *   *

"BEST" MODEL

DEP VAR: Y   N: 17   MULTIPLE R: .978   SQUARED MULTIPLE R: .956

ADJUSTED SQUARED MULTIPLE R: .946   STANDARD ERROR OF ESTIMATE: 0.698

VARIABLE	COEFFICIENT	STD ERROR	STD COEF	TOLERANCE	T	P (2 TAIL)
CONSTANT	13.626	0.866	0.000		15.734	0.000
X5	2.457	0.815	1.190	0.0217194	3.015	0.010
X12	-3.263	0.781	-1.687	0.0207675	-4.181	0.001
X13	-1.425	0.266	-0.506	0.3810741	-5.367	0.000

ANALYSIS OF VARIANCE

SOURCE	SUM-OF-SQUARES	DF	MEAN-SQUARE	F-RATIO	P
REGRESSION	137.554	3	45.851	94.195	0.000
RESIDUAL	6.328	13	0.487		

*   *   *

SECOND BEST MODEL

DEP VAR: Y   N: 17   MULTIPLE R: .955   SQUARED MULTIPLE R: .912

ADJUSTED SQUARED MULTIPLE R: .891   STANDARD ERROR OF ESTIMATE: 0.988

VARIABLE	COEFFICIENT	STD ERROR	STD COEF	TOLERANCE	T	P (2 TAIL)
CONSTANT	9.668	0.771	0.000		12.534	0.000
X5	4.468	1.336	2.165	0.0162032	3.344	0.005
X12	-4.358	1.083	-2.253	0.0216331	-4.022	0.001
X22	-1.623	0.580	-0.839	0.0754906	-2.799	0.015

ANALYSIS OF VARIANCE

SOURCE	SUM-OF-SQUARES	DF	MEAN-SQUARE	F-RATIO	P
REGRESSION	131.185	3	43.728	44.770	0.000
RESIDUAL	12.697	13	0.977		

*   *   *

THIRD BEST MODEL

DEP VAR: Y   N: 17   MULTIPLE R: .927   SQUARED MULTIPLE R: .859

ADJUSTED SQUARED MULTIPLE R: .838   STANDARD ERROR OF ESTIMATE: 1.206

VARIABLE	COEFFICIENT	STD ERROR	STD COEF	TOLERANCE	T	P (2 TAIL)
CONSTANT	9.985	0.931	0.000		10.729	0.000
X5	2.581	1.407	1.250	0.0217370	1.834	0.088
X12	-4.148	1.318	-2.145	0.0217370	-3.146	0.007

ANALYSIS OF VARIANCE

SOURCE	SUM-OF-SQUARES	DF	MEAN-SQUARE	F-RATIO	P
REGRESSION	123.531	2	61.766	42.490	0.000
RESIDUAL	20.351	14	1.454		

*   *   *

FOURTH BEST MODEL

DEP VAR: Y   N: 17   MULTIPLE R: .982   SQUARED MULTIPLE R: .964

ADJUSTED SQUARED MULTIPLE R: .953   STANDARD ERROR OF ESTIMATE: 0.653

VARIABLE	COEFFICIENT	STD ERROR	STD COEF	TOLERANCE	T	P (2 TAIL)
CONSTANT	12.894	0.919	0.000		14.025	0.000
X5	3.333	0.923	1.615	0.0148244	3.612	0.004
X12	-3.501	0.744	-1.810	0.0200205	-4.706	0.001
X13	-1.195	0.283	-0.424	0.2928809	-4.217	0.001
X22	-0.737	0.437	-0.381	0.0580195	-1.686	0.118

ANALYSIS OF VARIANCE

SOURCE	SUM-OF-SQUARES	DF	MEAN-SQUARE	F-RATIO	P
REGRESSION	138.766	4	34.692	81.367	0.000
RESIDUAL	5.116	12	0.426		

*   *   *

FIFTH BEST MODEL

DEP VAR: Y   N: 17   MULTIPLE R: .965   SQUARED MULTIPLE R: .931

ADJUSTED SQUARED MULTIPLE R: .908   STANDARD ERROR OF ESTIMATE: 0.910

VARIABLE	COEFFICIENT	STD ERROR	STD COEF	TOLERANCE	T	P (2 TAIL)
CONSTANT	11.761	1.349	0.000		8.718	0.000
X5	3.114	1.437	1.508	0.0118798	2.167	0.051
X12	-3.093	1.215	-1.599	0.0145941	-2.547	0.026
X15	-0.608	0.333	-0.216	0.4097954	-1.826	0.093
X22	-1.340	0.556	-0.693	0.0696088	-2.410	0.033

ANALYSIS OF VARIANCE

SOURCE	SUM-OF-SQUARES	DF	MEAN-SQUARE	F-RATIO	P
REGRESSION	133.945	4	33.486	40.435	0.000
RESIDUAL	9.938	12	0.828		

*   *   *

SIXTH BEST MODEL

DEP VAR: Y   N: 17   MULTIPLE R: .945   SQUARED MULTIPLE R: .892

ADJUSTED SQUARED MULTIPLE R: .867   STANDARD ERROR OF ESTIMATE: 1.093

VARIABLE	COEFFICIENT	STD ERROR	STD COEF	TOLERANCE	T	P (2 TAIL)
CONSTANT	17.909	4.031	0.000		4.443	0.001
X5	2.162	1.293	1.047	0.0211701	1.672	0.118
X12	-3.333	1.262	-1.724	0.0194954	-2.642	0.020
X18	-1.975	0.982	-0.288	0.4045673	-2.010	0.066

ANALYSIS OF VARIANCE

SOURCE	SUM-OF-SQUARES	DF	MEAN-SQUARE	F-RATIO	P
REGRESSION	128.357	3	42.786	35.826	0.000
RESIDUAL	15.525	13	1.194		

Bibliography

Selected Bibliography and Reading List

Atkinson, John W. **An Introduction to Motivation**. Princeton, NJ: Van Nostrand, 1964.

Blake, Robert R., and Jane S. Mouton. **The Managerial Grid**. Houston, TX: Gulf, 1964.

Briggs Myers, Isabel, and Peter B. Myers, **Gifts Differing**. Palo Alto, CA: Consulting Psychologists Press, 1980.

Clemens, John K., and Douglas F. Mayer. **The Classic Touch: Lessons in Leadership from Homer to Hemingway**. 2nd ed. Lincolnwood, IL: NTC/Contemporary Books, 1999.

Clemmer, Jim. **Pathways to Performance**. Rocklin, CA: Prima Publishing, 1995.

Fleishman, Edwin, E.F. Harris, and H.E. Burtt. **Leadership and Supervision in Industry**. Columbus, OH: Bureau of Educational Research, The Ohio State University, 1955.

Hammer, Allen L. **Introduction to Type: A Description of the Theory and Applications of the Myers-Briggs Type Indicator**. Palo Alto, CA: Consulting Psychologists Press, 1992.

Follet, Mary Parker, 1868-1933. **Dynamic Administration**. New York, NY: Harper & Row, 1940.

Hamel, Gary, and C.K. Prahalad. "The Core Competence of the Corporation." **Harvard Business Review**, May-June 1990, pp. 79–91.

Homer. **The Iliad**. Trans. Samuel Butler, 1835-1902. Urbana, IL: Project Gutenberg, 2000.

Jackson, Douglas N. **Personality Research Form Manual**. Port Huron, MI: Research Psychologists Press, 1984.

Levitt, Theodore. "Marketing Myopia." **Harvard Business Review**, July-August 1960, pp. 45–46.

Machiavelli, Niccolo, 1469-1527. **The Prince**. Trans. W.K. Marriott. Urbana, IL: Project Gutenberg, 1998.

Maslow, Abraham H. **Motivation and Personality**. New York, NY: Harper, 1954.

McNeilly, Mark. **Sun Tzu and the Art of Business: Six Strategic Principles for Managers**. New York, NY: Oxford University Press, 1996.

Miller, Arthur. **Death of a Salesman: Certain Private Conversations in Two Acts and a Requiem**. New York, NY: Viking Press, 1949.

Murray, Henry Alexander. **Explanation in Personality**. New York, NY: Oxford University Press, 1938.

Nolan, John. **Confidential: Uncover Your Competitors' Top Business Secrets Legally and Quickly—and Protect Your Own**. New York, NY: HarperBusiness, 1999.

Plato, circa 428-347 B.C. **The Republic**. Trans. Benjamin Jowett, 1817-1893. Urbana, IL: Project Gutenberg, 1994.

Plutarch, circa 45-125 A.D. **Lives of the Noble Grecians and Romans**. Trans. Arthur Hugh Clough, 1819-1861. Urbana, IL: Project Gutenberg, 1996.

Sandy, William. **Forging the Productivity Partnership**. New York, NY: McGraw-Hill, 1990.

Shakespeare, William, 1564-1616. **King Lear**. Urbana, IL: Project Gutenberg, 1997.

Sophocles, circa 496-406 B.C. **Oedipus Trilogy**. Urbana, IL: Project Gutenberg, 1992.

Sun Tzu, circa 6th century B.C. **The Art of War**. Urbana, IL: Project Gutenberg, 1994.

Thoreau, Henry David, 1817-1862. **Walden**. Urbana, IL: Project Gutenberg, 1995.

Tuckman, Bruce W. "Developmental Sequences in Small Groups." **Psychological Bulletin**, Vol. 54, 1965, pp. 229–249.

Index

Accounting principles and standards, 98, 102, 103, 137, 138

Allen, Robert, 85

American Dream, 81, 133-135, 137-138, 139
    capital obstacle to, 133-135
    government as most visible obstacle to, 137-138
    labor obstacle to, 133-135
    leadership obstacle to, 133-135

American values, 81, 106

"American Welfare," 98

Anemic national savings rate, 83

Askew, Reubin, 133

Associate Retention and Motivation Strategies (ARMS), 129

AT&T, 29, 85

Attracting, Retaining, Motivating (ARMing) Project, 121-132

Bauman, Michael, 47